FACING CHANGE

Strategies for Problem Solving in the Congregation

Joseph S. Zaccaria

AUGSBURG Publishing House • Minneapolis

FACING CHANGE
Strategies for Problem Solving in the Congregation

Copyright © 1984 Augsburg Publishing House

All rights reserved. Except for brief quotations in critical articles or reviews, no part of this book may be reproduced in any manner without prior written permission from the publisher. Write to: Permissions, Augsburg Publishing House, 426 S. Fifth St., Box 1209, Minneapolis, MN 55440.

Scripture quotations unless otherwise noted are from the Revised Standard Version of the Bible, copyright 1946, 1952, and 1971 by the Division of Christian Education of the National Council of Churches.

Library of Congress Cataloging in Publication Data

Zaccaria, Joseph S.
    FACING CHANGE.

    Bibliography: p. 111
    1. Christianity—20th century.   2. Church management.
3. Change—Religious aspects—Christianity.
I. Title.
BR121.2.Z28   1984   254   84-18552
ISBN 0-8066-2097-8

Manufactured in the U.S.A.   APH 10-2156

1 2 3 4 5 6 7 8 9 0 1 2 3 4 5 6 7 8 9

Contents

Preface   5

Part 1: Introduction and Overview   7
1   The Congregation at the Crossroads   9
2   Moving out of the Intersection   21

Part 2: A Method for Problem Solving   35
3   Integrated Problem Solving   37
4   The Readiness Phase: See and
    Understand   48
5   The Preparatory Phase: Reflect
    and Focus   63
6   The Implementation and Evaluation
    Phase: Act and Review   75

Part 3: Variations   87
7   Variations in the Method   89
8   Developing a Proper Balance   100

Bibliography   111

Preface

The church as congregation is truly a unique phenomenon. It is simultaneously secular and spiritual in quality. Moreover, it is *in* the world, but it is not *of* the world. It must confront the problems of organizations in general. Yet, mindful of its spiritual heritage, the church as congregation must often develop some very special coping mechanisms for ensuring its continued growth and development.

The contemporary congregation faces some very real and critical challenges. Depending upon one's point of view, the church and its component congregations are either in a state of serious imminent crisis or in an opportune position to extend and enrich existing ministries to a higher level of service to God and humankind. A danger of overstating problems is that the church as congregation may become unnecessarily debilitated. It may thereby become immobilized, unable to develop effective action. On the other hand, a danger of understating the importance of some very real problems is that the church's response may be inadequate and thus contribute to more serious problems in the future. Located between these extremes is a truly wide range of realistic perceptions and effective responses to the broad array of problems in the ongoing life of the congregation.

Central to this total situation is the phenomenon of change. Change is both complex and many-faceted. It is confrontational and potentially exhausting. It activates and creates concern. It is sometimes threatening; yet it has the potential for creating Christian enlightenment. Change includes elements of doubt and fear coupled with elements of hope and inspiration. The major theme of this book is that the contemporary congregation is standing at a crossroads. Moreover, it is being confronted by the complex phenomenon of change. Change processes are creating both crises and opportunities. The congregation cannot avoid the powerful forces of change. Indeed, the response to change may determine the future vitality of the church as an institution and the future viability of any given congregation as an organization.

Part 1: Introduction and Overview

Part 1 of this book is primarily introductory. It first describes some selected aspects of the nature of change and the pressures that change is creating for the local congregation. The congregation is viewed as being situated at a crossroads from which each road will lead the congregation to a different location. The congregation cannot remain at the crossroads. It must choose a direction and a course of action for dealing with change and for moving out of the junction. In this regard, a number of potential options are explored. Some growth-retarding and some growth-promoting strategies are presented.

The intent of this portion of the book is twofold: (1) to sensitize the reader to a unique perspective on the forces operating on the contemporary congregation and (2) to point the direction for some positive approaches for dealing with the challenge of change. Problem solving is seen as a central process for dealing with change. It is an inherent aspect in the functioning of virtually every working group within the congregation. Finally, this section highlights the fact that the *challenge* of change is for the congregation to use an appropriate problem-solving technology as a means for service to God and humankind.

1 The Congregation at the Crossroads

Adam: *Well, Eve, I guess it's too bad that we have to leave this wonderful garden.*
Eve: *Yes. I have an uncomfortable feeling that we are entering a period of change.*

Introduction

In a very real sense, the Bible is a historical account of the changing relationship between God and humankind. Beginning with a description of the creation of the world, it then tells of the creation of Adam and Eve and their harmonious relationship with each other, their environment, and God. After their sin, however, the fundamental God–human being relationship is altered. A major emphasis throughout the Old Testament is the evolving pattern of the relationship of the Chosen People with their God. Throughout this unfolding account of the Old

Covenant relationship is an expectant yearning for a promised Messiah. After that Messiah came to earth, the Gospels highlighted another profound change in the God–human being relationship. Christ's long road to Calvary, his crucifixion, his resurrection appearances, and his ascension each represented a profound change in the nature of the God–humankind relationship.

Eventually the early New Testament church emerged as individual Christians banded together to form closely knit informal groups. Later on, the process of change continued in the rise of the Roman Catholic church, the Reformation, the spread of Protestantism, the many struggles within the Christian church, and, more recently, a period of uneasy discourse among and between the many factions within the Christian church. This growing ecumenical movement appears to herald further profound changes within Christendom.

Paralleling these changes is a similar and more marked series of societal changes and evolving patterns of secular life. A broad array of technological, political, economic, educational, work, and family changes have dramatically altered our general standard of living and our quality of life. Today the church as an institution and congregations as organizations share a characteristic with other societal institutions and organizations—they are being confronted by a series of overwhelming changes.

A significant aspect of these changes is that they have created challenges in virtually all of the important domains of life:

1. How can we maintain peace in a world in which the threat of atomic war is still used as a suicidal extension of politics?
2. How can we deal with the social and political implications of the world's growing population when, with every effort of aid, we are faced with an avalanche of new and hungry mouths?
3. How can we develop a closer cooperation between the races of humankind when we continue to encounter political states addicted to obsolete nationalism and ethnocentric isolation?
4. How can we deal with the massive encroachment of automation and the resulting problems of technological displacement when we have an uneven race between people and machines for jobs that machines can do better?
5. How can we more effectively increase human mental processes to handle greater and greater tasks as lesser tasks are taken over by automation?
6. How can we keep our total educational system in tune with our technological society, effectively shifting from the forced feeding of facts to the improvement of useful mental digestion?
7. How can we effectively deal with the grim and grisly skeletons of crime and juvenile delinquency hiding in the closets of American society?
8. How can we deal with those defectors from human society who escape reality through drug addiction and alcoholism?
9. How can we effectively deal with the fouling of our environment through acute air pollution and the contamination of our lakes, rivers, and streams?

10. How can our form of government better deal with the pressing and increasingly complex problems of a technological scientific revolution?
11. How can we improve the rapidly fading American image abroad?
12. How can we rationally deal with irrational forces militantly united in their opinion that our society is responsible for the world's injustices?
13. How can we effectively deal with the information explosion?
14. How can we discourage the flood of re-hashed, duplicated trivia ground out in millions of pages for a public that does not have the time, interest, or vocabulary to read it?
15. How can we effectively deal with the threat of old age despondency and human junk-yards as more and more people live longer and longer and retire younger?
16. How can we prevent those over 65 from being excommunicated from constructive social participation?
17. How can we open our congested cities and let the traffic move through more quickly?
18. How can we furnish water for the parched and arid areas of the earth that at present will not sustain agriculture?
19. How can we eliminate the ravages of disease and old age?
20. How can we better understand the universe about us, under us, and within us?

In recent years there has been a growing sense of concern and alarm within the church. Congregations are in a state of stress. Throughout our society, change has created an unsettling restlessness within many congregations:

1. Church attendance is, in general, decreasing.
2. Congregational members are experiencing increasingly serious psychological, vocational, economic, and family problems.
3. The church appears to be playing a less significant role in the life of a growing segment of the population.
4. Congregations are being encumbered with increasingly serious financial problems.
5. Neighborhoods and communities of which churches are a part are confronted by a wide range of problems.

In short, the church may be in the process of being moved to the nonproductive edge of an increasingly secularized society.

But change is not new. It is an inherent aspect of the human condition. In the past change was relatively slow, predictable, and manageable. Today, however, the quality, quantity, rate, and scope of change are both dramatic and potentially overwhelming. In his book *Future Shock* Alvin Toffler described the current situation as follows:

> We have in our time released a totally new social force—a stream of change so accelerated that it influences our sense of time, revolutionizes the tempo of daily life and affects the very way we "feel" the world around us. . . . We must learn how to alter the texture of existence (p. 3).

The many faces of change

At first glance the concept of change appears to be deceptively simple. It seems obvious that change is occurring all around us. Even the most casual observer can readily identify numerous examples of change. It is this ever-present quality, however, that tends to numb our senses to the immense proportion of the change phenomenon. More importantly, this numbness and insensitivity can lead a congregation (including its leaders) to overlook the need to consider change and its implications for the ongoing life of the congregation. It is important, therefore, that we as Christians be sensitive to change, understand its dynamics, and make appropriate responses to this many-faceted phenomenon.

Change as a force

Change is a force—a dynamic force. It comes in part from within people. It comes in part from between and among people. It comes in part from the environment, i.e., the society in which we live. Change as a force interacts with another set of forces, namely, forces for stability. Much of the stress and strain within and on a congregation stems from the interplay of the forces of change and the forces of stability.

Change as a demand

As congregational members sense the force of change, that force creates a set of demands or expectations. Some demands on the congregation arise from individual people—both inside and outside of the congregation. Other demands arise from a variety of types of family living units. An even broader set of demands arises from the neighborhood, the community, society, and from the world family of nations. These demands or expectations are made known to a congregation in the form of expressions of need:

1. Basic needs of life such as food, clothing, and a place to live.
2. Psychological needs such as love and esteem.
3. Social needs such as caring, belonging, and self-esteem.
4. Economic needs such as the need to provide for the financial welfare of a family living unit.
5. Spiritual needs such as developing a sense of meaning and purpose.

Both as a societal organization and as the gathered people of God, a congregation is expected to help in meeting these demands or needs. To be sure, the congregation cannot meet all of the varied and often incompatible sets of demands. On the other hand, to the extent that any given congregation does not make some type of contribution to the demands and expectations created by the forces of change, it runs the very real danger of becoming an irrelevant and dying organization.

Change as a crisis

As a congregation becomes aware of the numerous demands placed on it, a crisis arises. A gnawing realization begins to grow. Members may become increasingly sensitive to the congregation's shortcomings, its inability to prevent the pain and sorrow brought on by the urgency of unmet needs. They may also sense the nature of other crises that abound both inside and outside of the walls of the seemingly tranquil church. As the crises inside and outside of the congregation grow, and as the understanding of these crises increases, the forces of change that became demands and crises create yet another crisis—a crisis of stress. This stress crisis emerges through a realization that there is a gulf between the rhetoric (or words) and the actions (or behaviors) of the congregation.

Change as a challenge

For a congregation the challenge of change is to make a positive contribution to needs, expectations, and demands from within and from without. Wallace E. Fisher (*A New Climate for Leadership*, Parthenon, 1976, p. 28) has summarized this point of view as follows:

> . . . working through the word [Christ] *calls* individuals, gathers them into Christ's new community [the church], *enlightens* them, *nurtures* them, and *motivates* them to *serve* God in the world.

The challenge of change is for the congregation to develop a sense of mission and a related set of ministries through which it can truly become an agent of God in the world.

Change as an opportunity

Jesus once spoke these words to his disciples: "The harvest is plentiful, but the laborers are few . . ." (Matt. 9:37). The harvest is even greater today than it was when those words were originally spoken. To be sure, the needs, expectations, demands, and crises are greater today than at any other time in history. So what is the nature of the opportunity?

The opportunity is a chance for individual Christians, for congregations, and for the church as a societal institution to serve God and humankind in a world filled with need.

- This should be our *mission.*
- This should be our *ministry.*
- This should be our *stewardship effort.*
- This should be our *program.*
- This should be our *life.*

Guided by love, *serving* God and humankind, *living* in Christ, *led* by the Holy Spirit, *aided* by the Word, and *supported* through prayer, we as the people of God have an opportunity to develop a richer life for ourselves through a combined individual, group, and congregational effort as God's agents in the world.

Change as a response

The ongoing life of a congregation may be viewed in part as a response to God's love, God's grace, and God's call. For example, Paul characterized the church as "the called one," writing: "To the church of God . . . called to be saints together . . ." (1 Cor. 1:2). A call naturally leads to a response. For individual Christians and for a congregation, the appropriate response consists of three parts:

1. Willingness—
   - to *hear* God's call,
   - to *obey* God's will,
   - to be *guided* by love,
   - to be *led* by the Holy Spirit.

2. Commitment—
   - to *love* God and humankind,
   - to *serve* God in the world.
3. Action—
   - to translate *faith* into *good works.*

Change as an outcome

The result of action is an outcome. A congregation that makes an appropriate response in an attempt to do God's will can stand on the many promises in the Word. From a God-centered congregational effort, we can know that we will achieve certain outcomes:

1. We can *live* in a right relationship with God by becoming *redeemed* from our sins (Titus 2:14), *reconciled* with God (Rom. 5:10), *justified* by faith (Rom. 3:28), and *sanctified* by the work of the Holy Spirit.
2. We can *advance* the kingdom of God (Matt. 6:33).
3. We can *enjoy* the fruit of the Spirit: love, joy, peace, patience, kindness, goodness, faithfulness, gentleness, and self-control (Gal. 5:22-23).
4. We can *contribute* to the development of a better world.
5. We can *fulfill* ourselves through service to others.

The situation at the crossroads

The sweeping changes in virtually all aspects of life have placed the Christian church and its congregations at the crossroads. We are at a junction and must make what appears to be a critical decision. For a congregation that decision involves making a commitment through its identity and sense of mission to move out of the intersection and to follow an appropriate course of action. The issue can be stated in the following way: *Given the many faces of change which are confronting each congregation, how will each congregation respond to the challenge of change?*

From a spiritual point of view the issue is: How can *this* congregation carry out its mission and how will *this* congregation become a vehicle for God in the change-filled world of today? From a secular point of view the issue emerges in the form of the following question: How will this congregation respond to forces, demands, crises, challenges, and opportunities created by the broad range of societal changes? At the outset it appears these issues invite the development of a new sense of mission, a set of congregational programs, and a response that reflects a compliance with God's will. While different congregations will make somewhat different responses due to their unique circumstances, an integrated spiritual–secular response is called for. This is because a congregation can best be understood as a holistic organization—both spiritual and secular in quality. To be sure, a congregation is primarily spiritual in nature. On the other hand, many of the same dynamics that operate in secular organizations clearly function within a congregation

The course of action of each congregation will be determined largely by its leaders—its pastoral leaders, its formal leaders, and its informal leaders. In a very real sense, the burden of responsibility rests with these people to determine the direction and the course of action that the congregation will take in order to move from the crossroads. Once the leadership of the congregation has determined the general direction(s) in which the congregation will go and has developed a specific plan of action, the burden of responsibility is partially transferred to the rest of the congregation to become committed to the decisions and to make a contribution to the chosen course and plan.

2   Moving out of the Intersection

See that you fulfill the ministry which you have received in the Lord (Col. 4:17).

Take heed that no one leads you astray (Mark 13:5).

As noted in the last chapter, the congregation is at a figurative crossroads. Confronted by the challenge of change, it must make some type of response. To be sure, once a congregation becomes aware of the need for change, it will make some type of response. There are three general responses that a congregation can make. The easiest is to *ignore* the need for change by continuing to do the same things through the same types of programs that the congregation has employed in the past. The second general response is to *resist* the need for change either by returning to older programs that have been previously discarded and replaced or by choosing to go in the wrong direction. The third option is to *comply* with God's will and serve others in a spirit of love.

The Bible describes numerous accounts of people who were touched by the forces of change and decided to ignore the need to change. For example, the story of the rich young man (Luke 18:18-25) details how Jesus challenged this man to follow him. The rich young man ignored the need to change and continued to live the life he had led prior to talking with Jesus. In effect, he ignored the challenge of Jesus. In Exodus 32 is an account of how the people of Israel had at first accepted the challenge of living in a harmonious relationship with God as reflected in the Old Covenant (the 10 Commandments) but then ignored God's will by returning to the old practice of worshiping idols—in this case a golden calf. Jonah is another excellent example. He was challenged by God to preach to the people of Nineveh, but he resisted by going in the wrong direction.

On the other hand, the Bible also illustrates how many people responded to the challenge of change by complying with God's will. Abraham and Moses responded to the challenge and became great leaders of the Israelites. Joshua and Gideon met their challenges and became military leaders. David and Solomon followed God's will and became kings of a great nation. Old Testament prophets such as Isaiah, Jeremiah, and Ezekiel complied with God's will, becoming spokespersons for God to a nation that turned deaf ears to God's messages and warnings. Noah, Joseph, Daniel, and numerous other Old Testament characters also followed the will of God. Likewise, in the New Testament there are many accounts of people who responded to the will of God: John the Baptist, the disciples, and the early apostles, for example, each faced the challenge of change, heard God's call, and in varying degrees complied by following God's will.

All of the above-named biblical characters had certain characteristics in common:

1. They lived during times of significant change.
2. Their lives were challenged by change.
3. They heard God's call to follow a certain course of action.
4. They responded to God's call and followed his will.
5. They made significant contributions to the advancement of God's kingdom and to humankind.

As human beings, however, each was imperfect. They did not completely comply with God's will.

People of God today, both as individuals and as congregations, are also confronted by both spiritual and secular challenges of change. We are at a crossroads that demands a response. Three general options are available: *ignore, resist,* or *comply.* It is hoped that congregational leaders will help congregations to be not merely "hearers of the word" but rather "doers of the word." It is hoped that individual Christians, congregations, and the institutional church will respond to the challenge of change in a manner parallel to the Israelite response to Joshua: "The Lord our God we will serve, and his voice we will obey" (Josh. 24:24).

The challenge of change for the Christian congregation is to follow the will of God by serving God and humankind. The best example of a life devoted to following the will of God is the life of Jesus. His life and ministry point the way for the contemporary congregation. The congregation should study his teachings and stand on his promises. A congregation is called to be an agent of God and his love in a world in need—a world yearning for hope, meaning, and ways to meet the many problems created by the forces of change. With a systematic intentional plan for implementing its mission, a congregation can develop the willingness, commitment, and action to make a difference in the world. In order to do this, however, a congregation must confront the person of Christ and his message. At an operational level, it must ask and answer some difficult questions. It must decide on a series of critical issues.

Some basic issues

The basic thrust of this book is that congregational leaders have been entrusted with the responsibility of setting the course that a congregation will follow as its response to the challenge of change. A specific problem-solving approach will be suggested as a basic framework to guide thought and action. Prior to describing this specific approach to problem solving, however, some basic issues will be briefly highlighted. The intent here is to consider some of the basic issues that confront congregational leaders once they are aware of the nature of change and decide that some type of response is required.

Which goals will be met?

There are many problems confronting a congregation. Because of limited resources, congregational leaders must select which of those many problems it will attempt to address. It is impossible to meet all of the challenges, needs, and expectations. Thus, congregational leaders will have to select certain goals and try to meet them. In selecting certain goals, however, other possible goals must be ignored.

Which general change strategy will be employed?

A strategy is a very broad, overall approach utilized by the congregation to cope with problems to which it intends to respond. Sometimes a congregation does not make a conscious and deliberate choice of strategy. When this occurs, the congregation tends to stumble along from one problem situation to another. This shortcoming can be avoided by making a conscious and deliberate choice to follow one of the strategic courses of action listed below:

1. A slow, evolutionary strategy
2. A rapid, revolutionary strategy
3. A systematic, planned strategy

Congregational leaders will profit from reviewing these alternative general strategies and making an intentional decision to employ one of them.

What type of effort will be used?

There are three types of efforts that a congregation may employ to bring about change: structural efforts, technical efforts, and behavioral efforts. *Structural efforts* attempt to modify the roles, relationships, and organizational structures in the congregation. Some examples of structural efforts include the following:

1. The addition, deletion, or replacement of church staff.
2. Changing the committee structure.
3. Centralizing or decentralizing the organization of the congregation.

Technical efforts consist of applying new technologies to deal with ongoing activities within a congregation. The basic intent of this type of action is to improve the technological efficiency and the effectiveness of the pastor(s), staff, and congregational members. Listed below are some examples of technological efforts:

1. Extending worship and evangelism efforts by utilizing a radio or TV ministry.
2. Purchasing improved equipment for the church secretary.
3. Computerizing the church records system.
4. Buying or renting buses and utilizing efficient routing schedules to help transport people to church.
5. Altering the church building to accommodate physically handicapped people.

The last type of effort is a *behavioral effort*. This course of action involves direct attempts to change the behavior of congregational members through training or through staff or program development. Examples of behavioral efforts include workshops, retreats, seminars, classes, prayer groups, Bible study groups, sharing groups, and social support groups.

Who will provide the leadership?

Traditionally Christian churches have relied on the clergy to provide leadership. In some denominations that leadership stems primarily from a central office. In other denominations leadership is expected solely from the pastor(s) of the church. An alternative pattern is for the congregational leadership to come from the membership, in which case the pastor(s) may serve in such capacities as facilitator, teacher, or consultant. Another pattern mirrors the trend toward participative leadership in the secular world. In this arrangement the leadership within the congregation is shared by the pastor(s) and lay leaders.

What type(s) of leadership style will be employed?

Figure 2-1 is an adaptation from "How to Choose a Leadership Pattern" by Tannenbaum and Schmidt (*Harvard Business Review*, May-June, 1973). It summarizes five different types of leadership styles. The two major features of leadership styles are that each style involves a different type of behavior on the part of the leader and likewise delineates a unique type of response on the part of those who are being led. If a *telling style* of leadership is employed, then the leader will decide what should be done and, in effect, force the followers to do what he or she has decided should be done. When using the *selling style*, the leader presents a course of action and then attempts to persuade or convince the followers to do what the leader has decided. If the *testing style* of leadership is employed, the leader presents an idea and assesses whether the followers are willing to proceed along the course of action proposed. The *consulting style* of leadership consists of the leader placing the responsibility for decision making and action on the followers but making himself or herself available to help them if they ask for help. Lastly, in the *joining style* the leader shares the responsibility for decision making and action by becoming a co-worker and colleague with the followers.

Given different people, different problems, and different situations, any of the above leadership styles may be appropriate. Many problem-solving groups experience difficulties in achieving their tasks when the leader chooses an inappropriate leadership style for the situation at hand.

Figure 2-1

The Continuum of Leadership Styles

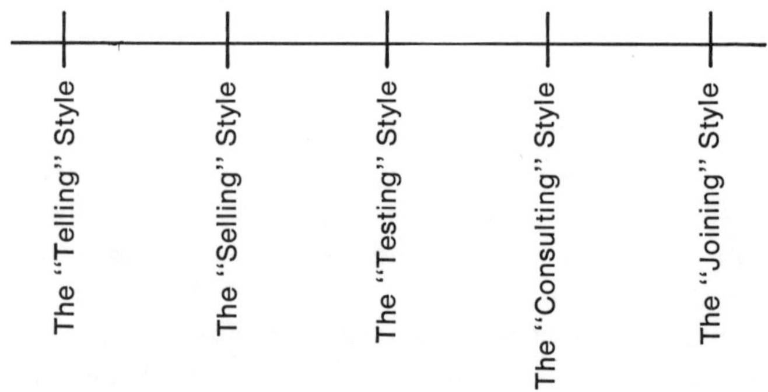

What will be the balance between stability and change?

The emphasis in this book is on change—change as a force, demand, need, expectation, crisis, challenge, opportunity, and response. A broad range of changes within a congregation and outside a congregation creates a sense of imbalance and urgency. It is important, however, to develop a healthy balance between change and stability. If too much change occurs, if change occurs too quickly, or if change occurs in too many areas of a congregation at the same time, then despite the fact that they may be well intentioned, the change efforts may be accompanied by harmful side effects such as resentment, confusion, and resistance. On the other hand, if there is too much stability in a situation where change is required, the congregation may become prone to stagnation, decay, lethargy, and despair. The congregation may become irrelevant to its members and the broader community of which it is a part. Finding the appropriate delicate balance between stability and change is one of the most important tasks for a congregation.

What specific responses will be made?

There are two categories of specific responses that can be made to the challenge of change. *Maladaptive* or *dysfunctional* responses are those types of action that impede the congregation's efforts to achieve its mission. Given that a change response is needed, some of the typical maladaptive or dysfunctional responses are listed below:

1. Denying the need to change
2. Using delaying tactics

3. Throwing out smoke screens
4. Oversimplifying the problem
5. Making the wrong types of changes
6. Blaming others
7. Carrying on nonproductive arguments
8. Exaggerating the seriousness of the problem.

Given that a change response is needed, an appropriate type of response is *renewal-oriented problem solving.*

1. The response should be *biblically based* or compatible with biblical precepts.
2. The response should be *intentional.*
3. The response should be *planned.*
4. The response should utilize effective *principles* from the social sciences: psychology, sociology, anthropology.
5. The response should involve *sound management practices.*
6. The response should meet huma*n needs.*
7. The response should further the *mission* of the congregation.
8. The response should be made in a spirit of *love.*
9. The response should comply with *God's will.*

A perspective on problem solving

The essence of problem solving is that change creates needs, demands, expectations, crises, challenges, and opportunities to which a congregation must respond. If any given problem is related to the mission of the congregation, it constitutes an instance in which the current congregational programs and activities are not achieving the goals of the congregation expressed in its mission. The major function of congregational leaders is to make the key decisions and to engage in a problem-solving effort aimed at eliminating or at least reducing the problem. Problem solving becomes the keystone in an intentional, systematic congregational effort to achieve goals. Each congregation is confronted with both developmental problems and situational problems.

Developmental problems

Over time, each congregation, like other organizations, has a somewhat predictable type of life history. In an article in the *Harvard Business Review* Gordon Lippitt and Warren Schmidt describe various stages and crises that developing organizations go through. Each stage or developmental phase in the life of a congregation is accompanied by certain general demands. These demands create predictable crises that are generated by the fact that the congregation has reached a new, higher, and more complex states of maturity. At each developmental stage in the life history of a congregation it is confronted with a different major developmental problem. If the congregation successfully copes with and masters that problem, it then moves on to the next higher stage of maturity and is then confronted with a new problem. In effect, it is only through confronting and resolving a series of major developmental problems that a church congregation becomes increasingly more mature, more effective in its ministries, and more respected within the community.

When a congregation is first formed, it faces the problem of *creation.* Its primary task is to develop the critical structures (e.g., committees) and processes (e.g., worship, Christian education, stewardship, etc.) that will enable it to begin its life. Once a congregation has been created and has developed its basic organizational structures and processes, it must then confront its next developmental task or problem, *survival*. It must struggle to survive in a community where other congregations and other organizations are competing with it for the time, talent, money, energy, and other resources of its members and its potential members. If the congregation is successful, it can become more mature by moving on to the next developmental stage with its major problem: *stability*. The congregation must develop a stable image and a stable existence. This is accomplished by determining its mission and evolving a set of relatively stable ministries.

When the congregation has proceeded this far, it has progressed to an organizational developmental stage comparable to adulthood. When the congregation has become stabilized, the next developmental problem is to earn a good *reputation*. It is through the development of a good reputation that a congregation can attract new members and gain additional resources for its ministries. A good reputation will nurture and reinforce the later efforts of the congregation in its attempts to grow and adapt to changing conditions. The next-to-the-last major developmental problem faced by a congregation in its history is to gain a capacity for *adaptability*. As changes occur inside and outside, a mature congregation is expected to be sensitive and develop flexible responses to change. Last, a very mature congregation is expected to confront the problem of *contribution*. As a mature congregation it must make a major contribution to the lives of its members and to the community of which it is a part. It must then maintain that contributing effort, or else it will stagnate.

As the congregation matures over time, and as it confronts each of the above stages of developmental tasks or problems, it must not only face the next problem, but it must continue to deal with the developmental problems that it has already mastered. The developmental problems that were faced at earlier developmental stages continue to require attention even though the congregation has become more mature and developmentally advanced.

Situational problems

Whereas the developmental problems that confront any given congregation are quite similar to the developmental problems facing other congregations at a similar stage in their life history, situational problems are unique to each congregation. Some types of situational problems are listed below.

1. *Structural problems* refer to difficulties arising from how the congregation is organized.
2. *Technical problems* arise in relation to how the congregation attempts to accomplish its major tasks such as worship, evangelism, service, etc.
3. *Personal problems* occur with individuals who are members of the congregation or members of various community groups.
4. *Social problems* emerge from the interpersonal relations among and between people.
5. *Financial problems* result from how a congregation, its members, or other community indi-

viduals and groups conduct their financial af-
fairs.
6. *Vocational problems* consist of difficulties relating to one's employment or unemployment.

Having considered the nature of change and some of the problems that it creates for a congregation, the remaining portion of this book is devoted to describing a specific problem-solving method—"integrated problem solving."

Part 2: A Method for Problem Solving

In operational terms, the challenge of change in the local congregation emerges in the form of problems — needs, demands, expectations, and crises — both inside and outside the congregation.

A useful way to think about problems is to divide them into three groups. *Technical problems* involve difficulties in the manner in which congregational ministries, activities, and programs are functioning. *Human problems* consist of individual, family, and group concerns. *Spiritual problems* constitute difficulties in such matters as faith, theology, and doctrine.

Working groups within a congregation are confronted by technical, human, and spiritual problems as they recognize existent shortcomings or as they anticipate the emergence of future difficulties. Having recognized a given problem, a working group then will deal with that problem through either a growth-promoting or a growth-retarding problem-solving effort.

Part 2 of this book highlights one of a number of problem-solving methods available to working groups within a congregation. Integrated spiritual-secular problem solving is an adaptation of a method advocated by William C. Morris and Marshal Shashkin (*Organization Behavior in Action,* West Publishing Co., 1976). It links elements of spiritual belief and action with the basic elements of Morris's and Shashkin's secular approach to problem solving. As a method of responding to the challenge of change, integrated problem solving consists of three major phases. Each phase is, in turn, subdivided into a number of steps that are implemented through the use of certain procedures and processes.

After the basic elements of integrated problem solving have been described in Part 2, Part 3 will consider some variations on this basic method that can be utilized in response to the unique circumstances and style of any given working group engaging in problem solving. Thus integrated problem solving constitutes a method that can be employed in its pure form or can be adapted or combined with other problem-solving methods in order to conform to the unique situation in which a given working group functions.

3 Integrated Problem Solving

Virtually all the biblical figures . . . used to describe the church emphasize an essential, living . . . relationship between Christ and the church. . . . If the church is the body of Christ — the means of the head's action in the world — then the church is an indispensable part of the gospel (Howard A. Snyder, *Community of the King,* InterVarsity, 1977, pp. 55-56).

All things should be done decently and in order (1 Cor. 14:40).

Congregational behavior as an expression of its identity

When an individual acts, that person does so as an expression of his or her identity, self-concept, or self-image. Behavior can thus be viewed as an outward expression of an inner set of attitudes, values, and beliefs collectively known as an identity, a self-concept, or a self-image. The total response of a congregation to the challenge of change is likewise an outward manifestation of its congregational identity, self-concept, or self-image. There are three general types of congregational self-images: singular images, multiple images, and integrated images.

The most simple type of image is a *singular congregational self-image*. When a congregation holds this type of image of itself, it adheres to one image as an expression of its identity. This image may be represented as a single circle, denoting that the image of the congregation can be encompassed within the space of that circle:

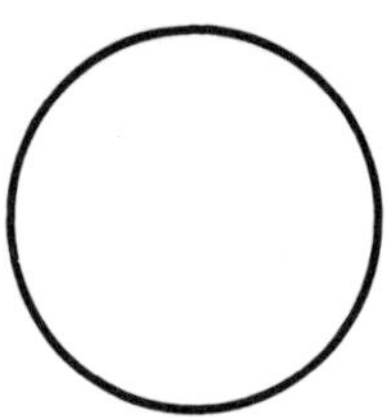

A singular congregational image may be derived from any one of many images of the church described in the Bible. Paul S. Minear, for example, has identified 53 Old Testament passages and 722 New Testament passages in which many different images of the church have been described (*Images of the Church in the New Testament*, Westminster, 1970). Some of the more commonly known images are listed below:

1. The body of Christ (1 Cor. 12:27)
2. People of God (Heb. 8:10)
3. Priesthood of believers (1 Peter 2:9)
4. Stewards (1 Peter 4:10)
5. Chosen people (1 Peter 4:10)
6. People of light (1 Thess. 5:5)
7. Salt of the earth (Matt. 5:13)
8. Temple of the living God (2 Cor. 6:16).

Other images are of the congregation as a soul-winning organization, a community of believers, or a family-oriented church. The central point of this discussion is this: The problems to which a congregation will attend are greatly influenced by the nature of its identity as a congregation.

When a congregation holds a *multiple congregational self-image*, it includes two or more images loosely linked together as illustrated below:

These images may be either spiritual or may include both spiritual and secular elements. Presumably, if the images are solely secular, then that congregation is not a congregation in any conventional sense of the term.

An *integrated congregational self-image* also is composed of multiple elements. Unlike the multiple congregational self-image whose elements are merely loosely linked, however, the components in the integrated self-image are functionally joined or fused together as illustrated below:

The congregational self-image and problem solving

A congregational self-image is like the lens of a photographer's camera—it enables the congregation to view itself and the world and to help it understand how it should function. A photographer may have telephoto lenses, wide-angle lenses, normal lenses, zoom lenses, close-up lenses, and/or a variety of filters and special lenses. Different lenses can be used to view a subject or a scene. Each lens will produce a somewhat different picture. A congregation's self-image thus has a descriptive function and a prescriptive function. It describes basic dynamics as well as the general direction that congregational life should follow and what type of outcome it will realize.

Whatever unique type of congregational self-image is held, integrated spiritual-secular problem solving offers a potentially useful contribution to the challenge of change. A congregation's self-image may consist, in part, of a problem-solving perspective. As such, a congregation may view itself as an organization that searches for, attends to, and attempts to resolve problems that are symptoms of its ministries that require change. This is the descriptive use of problem solving for the congregation. The prescriptive use of problem solving emerges as congregational leaders and members use problem solving as a means for carrying out the congregational mission.

Congregational life and integrated spiritual-secular problem solving

Figure 3-1 illustrates how integrated problem solving can be a component in the underlying beliefs of a congregation and in that congregation's response to the challenge of change. Numerous books have been written on virtually every component in figure 3-1. Congregations vary somewhat with respect to the nature and definitions of the components. They even hold differing conceptions of the underlying dynamics. It would appear, however, that virtually all Christian congregations will agree that each of the components in figure 3-1 are to some degree important to their ongoing life. Given the obvious wide range in beliefs and responses (action) within the Christian church, the following general summary is somewhat representative of the main line of belief, represented by the top portion of figure 3-1. The bottom portion of figure 3-1 represents the more idiosyncratic view of this writer regarding how problem solving can fit into the overall scheme of a congregation's response to change.

Following the rationale described above, the congregational response to the challenge of change occurs within the context of a set of underlying *basic beliefs,* which are embodied in the congregation's *identity* or self-image, which, in turn, lead to a *response.* The main thrust of figure 3-1 is as follows: The foundation of Christian belief rests on the *Trinity* or triune God (Father, Son, and Holy Spirit). Because of God's *love* for humankind, we receive *grace.* By God's grace we are *redeemed* from our sin, we are *reconciled* and *justified,* and we can lead *sanctified* lives. God's grace is a free gift that we acknowledge by confessing our faith in God's Son Jesus, who died on the *cross* for our sins. Through God's grace, Jesus' death, and our faith, we have *salvation* and thereby become *new creatures* (creations). As new creatures we can live in a right relationship with God, i.e., we are redeemed, reconciled, justified, and sanctified. Moreover, we can live a new kind of life—a life based on *faith* and a life devoted to doing *good works.*

Given that there are many different kinds of good works and given that change has created many needs, crises, demands, and expectations both within a congregation and outside it, a congregation's identity or self-image strongly influences which of the many problems confronting it will receive its attention. A congregation's *mission*—its vision of purpose—selectively leads that congregation to ignore some problems and to attempt to deal with others. Some type of intentional, systematic, and planned *problem solving* is useful both in relation to the congregation's identity as an organization that deals with problems

Figure 3-1

A Flow Chart
of Congregational Beliefs, Problems, and Action

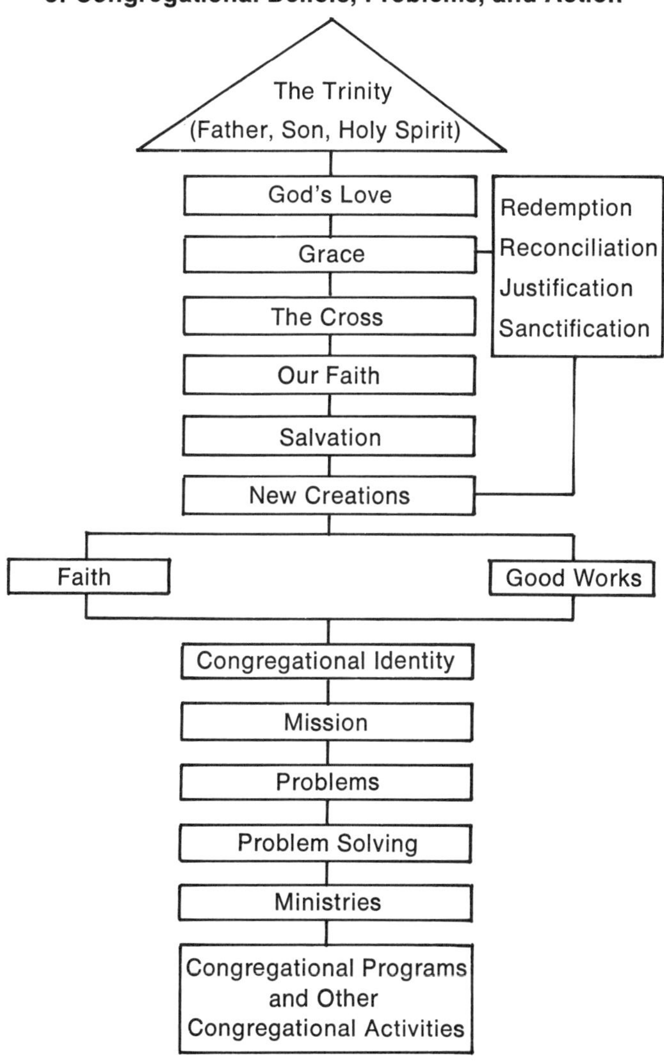

and in relation to response, i.e., as a method for helping to implement its *ministries,* its *programs,* and its other *activities.*

Integrated problem solving: an overview

Much of the progress of humankind has resulted from our capacity to adapt to changing situations through problem solving. In the past several centuries progress has often occurred as a result of using the scientific method. This method can be summarized as follows:

1. Understanding and defining a problem
2. Developing hypotheses
3. Testing hypotheses
4. Designing and carrying out an experiment
5. Evaluating the results
6. Returning to the problem, if necessary

Integrated problem solving is a spiritually sound, practical, and effective approach for enabling a congregation to meet the challenge of change. This approach links the basic elements of Christian faith and identity with a specific way of applying the scientific problem-solving method, and draws on knowledge from the social sciences such as psychology, sociology, and anthropology. It is critical, of course, that a congregation maintain a steadfast adherence to its fundamentally spiritual nature. Nevertheless, within this basic view of a congregation as a spiritual entity, it is useful at times to employ the knowledge and selected practices of science to further the mission and ministries of the congregation. Moreover, this type of spiritual-secular approach neither dilutes the basic faith and identity of a congregation nor does it in any way compromise the basic tenets or appropriate actions of a congregation's ministry within the Christian church. Rather, many congregations could incorporate this problem-solving method as an integral aspect of decision making and action with beneficial results.

Integrated problem solving consists of several phases or stages. Each phase or stage is divided into a series of steps. Each step, in turn, is carried out by using certain procedures and related processes. This method not only prescribes what should be done to deal with a problem, but it also identifies the traps and pitfalls of other problem-solving methods and prescribes how to avoid them. Thus, there is a clear differentiation between the stages, the steps, the procedures to be followed, the pitfalls of each step, and the process to follow in order to avoid the pitfalls. Integrated problem solving is summarized in table 3-1.

The Christian church is a societal institution. It is organized within two broad traditions—Protestantism and Catholicism. Within each of these traditions there are many diverse subgroupings. Yet despite this wide diversity it is bound together by a unifying allegiance to a triune God and by a unique relationship with that God. Given this diversity of circumstances in which congregations function, there is a range of appropriate types of responses to the challenge of change. It is the intent of this writer to describe one unique approach. It is not a universal solution for all problems of church congregations; it is one possible method for responding to change. Thus, this method is appropriate for some congregations; it is inappropriate for use by other congregations; still others may choose to combine some elements of this method with aspects of one or more other methods.

Integrated problem solving can be used by a variety of problem-solving groups in the congregation such as the church staff, the board of elders or church council, a group of Sunday school teachers, or any of the many committees that function within the congregation. Even though there may be some variations in the general problem-solving style employed by different problem-solving groups, this method advocates a rather strict adherence to the specified series of phases, steps, procedures, and processes. Each of the following three chapters will describe one of the major phases or stages in the method.

Table 3-1
A Summary of Integrated Problem Solving

The Readiness Phase (See and understand)
    Step 1: Become aware of the problem
            a. Develop a proper mind-set
            b. Scan the congregation and the environment
            c. Gather information
            d. Evaluate the information
            e. Identify patterns
            f. Define the problem
               1. Symptoms
               2. Underlying causes
    Step 2: Understand the problem
            a. Understand the problem in general
            b. Understand the specific nature of the problem

The Preparatory Phase (Reflect and focus)
    Step 3: Clarify how the problem relates to the mission of the congregation
        a. Clarify the identity of the congregation
        b. Clarify the mission of the congregation
        c. Link the problem to identity and mission
    Step 4: Develop a set of expected outcomes
        a. Develop a clear statement of desired outcomes
        b. Develop a set of enabling objectives
    Step 5: Generate a range of alternative courses of action
    Step 6: Select a trial course of action

The Implementation and Evaluation Phase (Act and (review)
    Step: Develop an evaluation plan
    Step: Prepare the congregation for change
    Step: Initiate a course of action
        a. Provide adequate resources
        b. Monitor progress
        c. Follow the plan unless there is clear evidence that the plan should be altered
    Step: Alter the intervention as necessary
    Step: Carry out the evaluation plan
    Step: Complete the intervention
    Step: Reexamine the problem situation
    Step: Recycle through the process as necessary

4 The Readiness Phase: See and Understand

Step 1: Become aware of the problem
Step 2: Understand the problem

Introduction

The first of the three major phases in integrated probelm solving is the readiness phase. In this phase, the working group (a congregational governing body such as a council, long-range planning committee, session, board, or consistory, or a congregational committee such as a pastoral call committee, building committee, or stewardship committee) carries out two major steps: becoming aware of the problem and gaining an understanding of the problem. These are, in turn, carried out through a prescribed series of procedures that will be described below. The key feature of the readiness phase is that the working group focuses on doing the basic groundwork for the later phases of preparing for and implementing the change.

Step 1: Become aware of the problem

Develop a proper mind-set

A mind-set is a perspective or a point of view. It involves a particular mental framework for viewing a congregation. The first procedure in the process of integrated problem solving consists of having the leaders and members of the working group develop a mind-set or mental attitude that prepares them to become productively involved in the problem-solving process. Some aspects of a helpful mind-set include the following:

1. Maintaining a continued effort toward spiritual growth, e.g., Bible study, personal devotions, prayer.
2. Understanding the problem-solving process.
3. Developing a personal commitment to ministry and stewardship.
4. Developing a clear grasp of responsibilities, tasks, and goals.
5. Understanding the current identity, mission, and programs in the congregation.

Most important of all, it is critical that the working group conceive of itself as a group whose major task is to solve problems. This involves the working group having a mind-set or mental image of itself not merely holding meetings but rather working at solving problems. At first this distinction may appear to be trivial. It is crucial, however, that the working group (problem-solving group) convene with the intention of working at solving problems instead of the more passive attitude of "attending a meeting."

Scan the congregation and the environment

This basic procedure consists of viewing the congregation and the environment in order to acquire useful information about how the congregation is functioning. The scanning or viewing is, in effect, a reconnaisance process. For example, each of the main activities in the ongoing life of a congregation should be viewed periodically in terms of how that aspect of congregational life is proceeding. A congregation may be viewed as a system, i.e., a network of interrelated groups (subsystems). Each of these groups should be reviewed periodically in order to determine the extent to which it is functioning well and contributing to the mission of the congregation. Figure 4-1 illustrates some of the major subsystems within a typical congregation. Since a church congregation does not function in a vacuum, it is also important to scan the environment within which the congregation operates: the neighborhood, community, state, nation, and world.

Gather and evaluate information

The purpose of scanning is to gather information— to keep one's finger on the "pulse" of what is happening in order to identify areas in which problems occur. The information gathered consists of problems, unmet needs, crises, etc., that can serve as guideposts to direct the problem-solving group to people, places, and events where problem solving is required. Consider, for example, the useful information that can be gathered from the following typical sources to

Figure 4-1

The Congregation as a System and Its Component Subsystems

The Congregation as a System

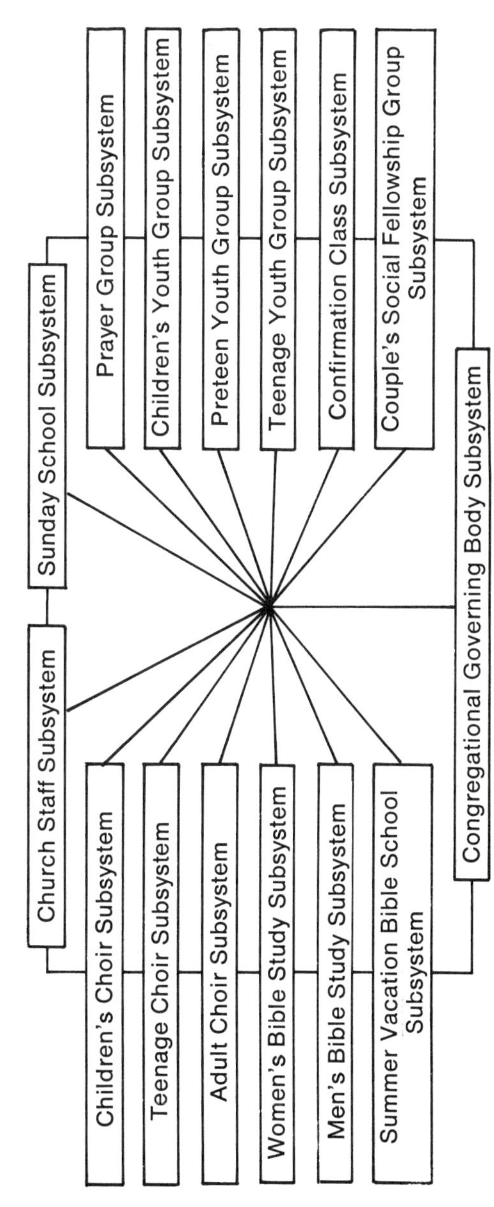

help evaluate the extent to which the congregation is achieving the goals related to its mission:

1. *Congregational Programs:*

   Evangelism   Property
   Worship   Christian education
   Stewardship   Youth
   Community service   Bible study
   Prayer groups   Music

2. *The Neighborhood:*

   Programs in other churches
   Poverty programs
   Hunger issues
   Needs of lonely people
   Needs of disillusioned people

3. *Congregational Members with Special Needs:*

   Single people   People who are ill
   Unemployed persons   Angry and conflict-
   People who are   ridden persons
      grieving   Single parents
   Divorced people   People overcome by
   Elderly members   despair
   People who are   People with disabilities
      home-bound   Poverty-stricken persons

4. *The Community, Nation, and World:*

   Missionaries
   Human service organizations
   Environmental groups
   Oppressed people
   Victims of natural disasters
   Community action groups

Identify patterns

When a specific problem is identified, that particular problem is very often just one aspect of a more complex series of problems and problem events. This is called a *syndrome*. When this is the case, a change may be required in a whole program of activities in the congregation. For example, if scanning, gathering of information, and evaluation of that information in the area of Christian education reveals that Sunday school attendance in general has declined significantly, then the whole Sunday school program as a subsystem should be dealt with. If, on the other hand, one family within the congregation is experiencing a specific type of problem in raising a teenager, and that problem is an isolated one, a new program in the congregation is not warranted. Rather, one member of the congregation may be able to help that family.

Define the problem

Having carried out the above procedures, the problem-solving group can then proceed to define the nature of the problem. In this regard, it is important to distinguish between two aspects of the problem: the *symptoms* of a problem and its underlying *causes*. The problem-solving group should make the above distinction as it attempts to understand the problem.

The symptoms of problems occur within the various subsystems of the congregation such as those listed in figure 4-1. More specifically, problems arise in terms of the various activities occurring within the congregation. Each congregation develops a somewhat unique pattern of activities known as a *performance structure* through which it attempts to achieve its goals. These activities may be described in terms of eight groups or types of *basic processes*.

1. *Task processes* are those activities that relate to the central mission of the congregation such as the following:
   - Worship
   - Sacraments
   - Christian education
   - Evangelism
   - Social service

2. *Maintenance processes* include those congregational activities that sustain and support the operation of the task processes:
   - Stewardship activities
   - Maintenance of the church building and grounds
   - Socialization of new members, e.g., confirmation classes

3. *Communications processes* involve the different activities that enable individual members and groups to make requests and to inform other individuals and groups within the congregation:
   - Church newsletters
   - Church bulletin
   - Annual report
   - Telephone calls
   - Letters and memos
   - Verbal communication during meetings

4. *Decision-making processes* consist of the various activities whereby the present and future directions of congregational events and programs are determined:
   - Pastoral decisions
   - Decisions by the church staff
   - Decisions by the congregational governing body
   - Decisions by various congregational committees

- Decisions by families in the congregation
- Decisions by individual members
- Decisions at congregational meetings

5. *Control processes* within the congregation attempt to influence the behavior of congregational members within certain designated types of appropriate behaviors.
   - Appropriate behaviors are prescribed in:
     1. Worship services
     2. Christian education classes
     3. Interpretation of Bible
     4. Confirmation classes
     5. Creed(s)
   - Negative sanctions (punishments) may be given:
     1. Being dropped from church roles
     2. Excommunication
     3. Visitations by church members

6. *Adaptation processes* are the efforts by the congregation to adjust and respond to the expectations, requests, and demands for congregational change:
   - Adaptation to factors within the congregation
   - Adaptation to factors outside of the congregation

7. *Coordination processes* are those activities that are intended to plan and schedule activities of various groups of congregational members:
   - Committee meetings
   - Announcements

8. *Conflict processes* consist of activities that involve disagreements within the congregation:
   - Conflict-causing activities
   - Conflict-reducing activities

The above basic processes of the performance structure constitute the activities that describe the "what occurs" aspect in the ongoing life of a congregation.

Supplementing and complementing the performance structure with its eight basic processes is an explanatory structure that consists of three components describing "how it occurs," i.e., how a congregation accomplishes its tasks. The three components of the explanatory structure are briefly described below.

1. *Expectation processes* consist of the ways in which the congregational members are influenced to behave in accordance with the basic beliefs of that congregation:
   - Formal written expectations
   - Informal unwritten expectations

2. *Interpersonal relationship processes* comprise the behaviors among and between congregational members:
   - Functional interpersonal relationships that enhance the ability of a congregation to achieve its mission
   - Dysfunctional interpersonal relationships that reduce or interfere with ability of a congregation to achieve its mission

3. *Resource utilization processes* are the activities through which the congregation employs its resources to achieve its mission:
   - Utilization of secular resources:

     | Time | Technology |
     | Talent | Materials |
     | Money | Knowledge |
   - Utilization of spiritual resources:

     The work of the Holy Spirit

     The power of prayer

The use of the Word as the Word of God
—the dynamic Word of power; the words
of Christ—the living Word that is the
most complete revelation of God; and
the Bible—the written Word.
The sacraments
Worship services

Step 2: Understand the problem

Understand the problem in general

Having defined the general nature of the problem in terms of where it is located within the congregation (in which aspect of the performance structure) and having defined the problem in terms of how it has emerged (in the explanatory structure), the next procedure is to gain a general understanding of the basic dynamics involved in the problem. There are many useful theories and many helpful approaches for understanding congregational dynamics. Among these is the stress-strain theory of Eugene Haas and Thomas E. Drabeck (*Complex Organizations*, Macmillan, 1973). According to this view, as long as the stabilizing forces operating in the congregation are strong and there are few strong change forces, then the life of the congregation tends to be harmonious and placid. But, as noted above, the forces of change can distrupt a congregation and create many different types of problems. The two major types of change forces are *stresses* and *strains*. Congregational stress occurs when the performance demands, i.e., the expectations placed on a congregation, do not match the way in which the congregation responds to those demands. There is always some degree of stress because there is never an exact match between demands on the congregation and the congregational responses to those demands. Much of the time in a typical congregation there is mild to moderate stress. On the other hand, when the stress reaches the moderate to high zone, the problems related to that zone of stress become both apparent and increasingly troublesome. There are two basic categories of stress. *Demand overload* occurs when the demands on a congregation exceed the current response pattern. *Demand deprivation,* on the other hand, occurs when the demands on the congregation are lower than the capacity of the congregation to respond to demands. Demand deprivation in congregational life is relatively rare, but it may occur in the following types of situations:

1. The congregation may have effective social service programs but may not be properly "tuned in" to how and where those services should be employed.
2. In a well-established congregation that has paid off the mortgage note on the church building, there may be more funds available than current operating expenses.
3. A congregation may have members who are willing and able to contribute to community needs but have an insufficiently ambitious social service program.

In a spiritually healthy congregation there can be no demand deprivation in the spiritual domain. Biblical expectations for both individual Christians and for congregations are very high. The areas of evangelism, social service, Bible study, prayer, Christian education, and stewardship are more typical areas in the congregation where demand deprivation may occur.

In addition to the forces of stress described above, there are also forces known as *strains* that can cause tensions and problems in the congregation. Strains occur when there is a wrong "fit" in the way the congregation as a system and its component parts relate with each other. Strains may appear in expectations, in interpersonal relations, and in the way in which congregational resources are utilized. Furthermore, in each of these three areas there may be any one or a combination of three types of strain:

1. *Inconsistencies* are strains that occur when the nature of appropriate action is clear but the actions of individuals or subsystems are sometimes appropriate and sometimes inappropriate.
2. *Ambiguities* are strains that occur when the types of appropriate expectations, interpersonal relationships, and use of congregational resources are not clear or are poorly understood.
3. *Disagreements* are strains that occur when individuals or subsystems within the congregation hold different expectations, develop problems in their interpersonal relationships, or argue about how the limited resources of the congregation should be utilized.

Strains in the form of inconsistencies, ambiguities, or disagreements, as well as various kinds of stresses, occur in both the secular and spiritual aspects of congregational life. An integrated stress-strain view of congregational dynamics makes the following assumptions:

1. A few congregational problems may be purely spiritual in quality.
2. A few congregational problems may be purely secular in quality.
3. The vast majority of congregational problems are neither solely spiritual nor solely secular; they are spiritual-secular.

Understanding congregational problems from an integrated spiritual-secular perspective involves viewing the congregation as an interlocking network of interdependent subsystems whose dynamics are primarily spiritual-secular. The term *spiritual-secular* implies that an appropriate understanding of congregational dynamics emerges from an understanding of three separate types of dynamics. It involves understanding the different qualities of both spiritual and secular dynamics in the relatively few instances when the ongoing dynamics are either purely spiritual or purely secular in nature. Most fundamentally, however, an integrated view envisions congregational dynamics as complex blends of spiritual and secular components. It is through understanding the unique blending of spiritual and secular elements that an integrated spiritual-secular understanding emerges.

Understand the specific nature of the problem

This procedure requires the problem-solving group to come to grips with the specific aspects of the problem. Stemming from an integrated stress-strain view, congregational problems may be understood as either stresses (overload or deprivation) or strains (inconsistencies, ambiguities, and/or disagreements). A common understanding and consensus should be sought by all members of the problem-solving group by *describing, discussing,* and *agreeing* on all the key aspects of the problem such as:

1. What are the specific symptoms of the problem?
2. What are the specific causes of the problem?
3. What is occuring in the problem?
4. Who is involved in the problem?
5. Where does the problem occur?
6. When does the problem occur?
7. How often does the problem occur?
8. How serious is the problem?
9. What factors maintain the problem?
10. What factors keep the problem from being solved?

Summary

In this phase of integrated problem solving, the problem-solving group has begun the problem-solving process by getting itself ready to deal with the problem. If the problem-solving group has done its work adequately, it has identified a problem area that requires group action and it has developed a consensus understanding regarding both the generalities and the specifics of the problem. It has, in effect, laid the foundation for the following two phases. The group has not only begun the process of eliminating or at least reducing the problem but has also attended to matters related to its own cohesion, morale, trust, rapport, and a continuing capacity to engage in an honest, sincere, open process of communication. In so doing, it will have made an excellent beginning in the total process of problem solving. As the group proceeds to the next phase, it will then begin to delineate a plan of action for dealing with the problem.

5 The Preparatory Phase: Reflect and Focus

Step 3: Clarify how the problem relates to the mission of the congregation
Step 4: Develop a set of expected outcomes
Step 5: Generate a range of alternative courses of action
Step 6: Select a trial course of action

Introduction

The steps, procedures, and processes that constitute the preparatory phase of integrated problem solving are important because they determine the eventual course of action the group will take. This phase begins when the problem-solving group has developed a clear understanding of the specific nature of the problem. By the end of this phase, the problem-solving group will have developed a plan of action that will enable it to move to the last phase, in which the plan will be implemented.

Step 3: Clarify how the problem relates to the mission of the congregation

Clarify the identity of the congregation

The congregation's identity consists of its basic view or image of itself. A sense of identity is critical because it is the wellspring from which the mission and the ongoing activities of the congregation flow. To the extent that the congregation has a coherent, explicit, and operational identity or image, that image can be a foundation for the life of the congregation. To the extent that a congregation does not have a well-developed self-image (identity), it is probable that it will flounder. However brief, it is important that each problem-solving group within the congregation devote some time to clarifying the identity of the congregation. In so doing, each group anchors its planning and planning-related activities in the congregation's identity and enables its decisions to be consistent with that self-identity. Moreover, in so doing, the problem-solving group can proceed along a course of action in which it will later consider the mission of the congregation and the mission of the problem-solving group and eventually link the problem and its plan with identity and mission.

A congregation's identity consists of varying amounts of two types of components: biblically derived components and theologically derived components. Some of the more commonly known biblically derived components were listed in Chapter 3 (p. 39).

Theologically derived components of a congregational self-image are identity statements reflecting a spiritual ideology. They are derived from Scripture or related to Scripture but are not Scripture *per se*. Among the many spiritual identities or images of the congregation are the following:

1. A covenant community
2. The corporate representative of God on earth
3. The fellowship of the concerned
4. The company of the committed
5. The reborn flesh and blood people who are God's agents of reconciliation

Even if the problem-solving group focuses on the identity of the congregation only very briefly, a consideration of identity is an important procedure because, as noted above, the mission of the congregation and the specific mission or task of that problem-solving group stem directly from the self-identity of the congregation.

Clarify the mission of the congregation

Two of the many meanings of the word *mission* are particularly important to integrated problem solving. Mission is a process of being *sent* for some purpose, as in the case of the great commission (Matt. 28:19). A second meaning of the word *mission* denotes that an individual, group, or organization takes on a *self-imposed* duty, responsibility, or obligation. The latter meaning of mission is often conceived of as a *response* to God's call or God's will. The missions of many congregations and working groups within those congregations often contain varying amounts of these two meanings of mission. Mission statements are, in effect, statements of purpose. They tend to be rather global and abstract statements of how a congregation views its *call* and its *response*. Some of the more common types of congregational mission statements are listed below:

1. A mission solely to evangelize
2. A mission primarily to evangelize, but evangelism is supplemented and complemented by other missions such as Christian education, worship, counseling, fellowship, and service (e.g., Don Abdon, *Training and Equipping the Saints,* Parish Leadership Seminars, 1977)
3. A mission to achieve three broad goals: the custodianship of the gospel, the care of persons, and the care of the earth (Fisher, *A New Climate for Leadership,* Parthenon, 1976)
4. An overall mission to carry out a set of four ministries: worship, learning, witnessing, and service (Lou Accola, "Types of Goals for Working Groups in the Congregation," 1980)

In this procedure the problem-solving group first briefly clarifies the mission of the congregation and then clarifies its own mission, which is more specific and more operationally defined than the congregational mission. For example, a committee within the congregation may have the mission of promoting spiritual growth within the family unit. Devoting time to this procedure insures that the problem-solving group has a clear understanding of how its mission relates to the broader overall mission of the congregation. It also helps to build high morale, develops group cohesion, and provides direction and thrust to the remaining portions of the problem-solving effort.

Link the problem to identity and mission

In this procedure the working group explicitly discusses how the problem at hand relates to identity and mission. Working in terms of "reverse logic," the group should discuss and develop consensus along the following lines:

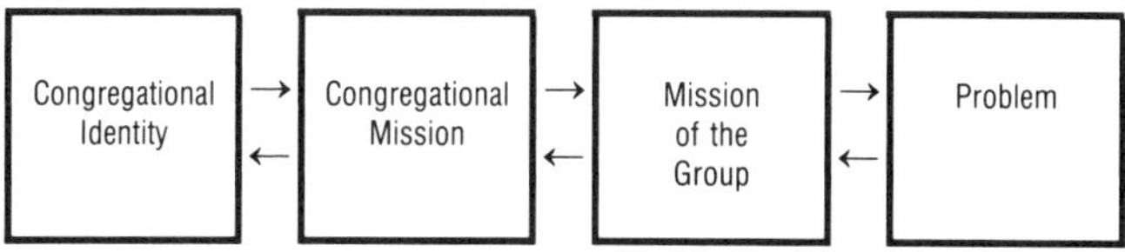

Step 4: Develop a set of expected outcomes

Often a problem-solving group such as a congregational governing body, committee, or task force attempts to do its work without adequately developing a clear set of goals. A long series of meetings may occur in which the group meanders along a winding path of indecisive action. In these cases, problem-solving efforts occur without a clear sense of either the direction in which the group is moving or an explicit idea of what the expected outcomes of the effort expended by the group are. The procedures in this step alleviate these problems by enabling the group to begin to focus its efforts.

Develop a clear statement of desired outcomes

This procedure requires the group to develop a reasonably explicit written statement of what should occur if the problem-solving effort is successful. In the case of the above situation regarding a need to promote spiritual growth within family units in the congregation, the statement of desired outcomes might be as follows: "There will be an increase in *(a)* the number of family units carrying on devotions together on a regular basis, *(b)* the number of family units attending worship services together, and *(c)* the quality of family relationships within the congregation." (Note: It is possible to develop even more specific terminal goals, e.g., a 20% increase in the number of family units carrying on devotions on a regular basis.)

Develop a set of enabling objectives

The desired outcomes statement describes what should be the final result of the work of the problem-solving group. In this procedure, the group develops a set of enabling objectives, i.e., a set of goals that it seeks as means for enabling the final desired outcomes to be realized. Thus, in the above case, the enabling objectives might be as follows:

1. To display 100 copies each of five pamphlets about family devotions and family worship in the narthex of the church.
2. To purchase 25 books on family devotions and family worship for the church library.
3. To inform members of available resources on family devotions and family worship.
4. To coordinate worship schedules and Sunday school schedules to enable families to attend Sunday worship services together.
5. To implement children's sermons that are five minutes in length at weekly Sunday worship services.

6. To implement two three-session classes on the topic of "Parent-Child Relationships."
7. To evaluate the effectiveness of the children's sermons.
8. To evaluate the effectiveness of the "Parent-Child Relationship" courses.
9. To evaluate the utilization of the pamphlets in the narthex and the books in the church library that focus on family devotions and family worship (Lou Accola, "Types of Goals. . . .").

The enabling objectives should be developed through a collaborative group effort. As is the case throughout the process to as great an extent as possible, group deliberations should be open, honest, and straightforward. It is critical that the enabling objectives be written in a form that is specific enough to serve as a guide for action in the later implementation phase. Several mnemonic devices have been developed to describe the qualities of good enabling objectives. They should be:

Specific		*Specific*
Measurable		*Concrete*
Achievable	*or*	*Attainable*
Realistic		*Measurable*
Timed		*Positive*

When this step has been completed, the problem-solving group will have developed statements of two sets of anticipated outcomes. One statement will describe the final results when the problem-solving process is complete (desired outcomes) and a second statement will delineate the outcomes that will be realized directly through the action of the group (enabling objectives).

Step 5: Generate a range of alternate courses of action

Most problem-solving groups make a serious error when deliberating on a course of action by selecting the first reasonable option rather than attempting to identify and select the best feasible course of action. In this step many alternative solutions are generated by encouraging all members of the problem-solving group to contribute their ideas. All ideas —good ideas and ideas that are not so good—should be accepted and listed without comment and without evaluation. This is the essence of brainstorming—a procedure designed to enhance the possibility of eventually developing a really good solution rather than settling for a solution that is merely satisfactory. The trap to avoid here is commenting, discussing, or evaluating ideas (at this point), because this will shut out group members' ideas and eliminate many potentially useful contributions. The intent here is to generate the widest possible range of all reasonable solutions.

Listed below are some alternative courses of action related to achieving each of the expected outcomes generated in the previous steps in this phase for the example cited above:

1. In order to promote family devotions on a more systematic basis:
   A. Provide families with helpful printed materials.

    B. Ask the pastor to preach one or more sermons related to family devotions.

    C. Teach a class on approaches to family devotions.
1. for parents
2. for children
3. for parents and children.

    D. Include family devotions as a topic in Sunday school classes.

2. In order to encourage families to worship together:

    A. Include a children's sermon in the worship service.

    B. Reschedule Sunday school so that children can attend worship services with their parents.

    C. Hold some special services
1. during week nights
2. on Sunday evenings

3. In order to help families within the congregation to be more spiritually linked with each other:

    A. Begin a family-based Sunday school class.

    B. Initiate a series of spiritual family support groups.

    C. Hold a series of potluck family dinners followed by some sharing experiences.

    D. During each worship service, briefly introduce a family to the congregation.

    E. Hold a brief social event after each Sunday morning worship service in which people can meet each other.

Step 6: Select a trial course of action

Having generated a list of alternative courses of action, the next step is to select the best alternative. The specific procedures in this step are listed below:

1. List the alternatives in written form.
2. Discuss each alternative course of action, delineating its advantages and possible benefits as well as its disadvantages and risks.
3. Evaluate the potential usefulness of each alternative.
4. Eliminate some alternatives.
5. Accept other alternatives.
6. Combine or revise other alternatives.
7. Decide on the most feasible total course of action in light of the current situation and the resources available.

Throughout the above procedures it is important to carry on group discussion and group deliberation in a way that members' ideas are not attacked. It is crucial that the members of the group do not become defensive and alienated because of a need to protect their ideas, their self-esteem, and their pride. The whole process of integrated problem solving should be characterized by honest, caring, sensitive, and constructive efforts by all members of the problem-solving group.

Following the problem described above — a need to promote more spiritual growth within the family unit—the group might complete this step by selecting the following alternative in light of the current situation and the available resources:

1. Contact chairpersons of Worship and Evangelism and Parish Education Committees requesting to be placed on committee agendas at the July 11 meeting.
2. Present program of "Ministry to the Family Unit" to Worship and Evangelism and Parish Education Committees on July 11.

3. Receive approval from church council to implement the program of "Ministry to the Family Unit" through recommendations from Worship and Evangelism and Parish Education Committees.
4. Research written resources on family worship and family devotions available in pamphlets and books from the national church offices, Bible bookstores, and libraries by September 1.
5. Collect available resources of pamphlets and books by September 15.
6. Arrange pamphlets in narthex of church by October 1.
7. Catalog collected books in the church library by October 1.
8. Present temple talks on "Family Worship and Family Devotions" and on available resources for family worship and family devotions at weekly Sunday worship services during August and September.
9. Print articles in monthly issues of the congregational newsletter during July, August, September, and October informing and encouraging utilization of available pamphets and books on family worship and devotions.
10. Print announcements in Sunday bulletins weekly during August, September, and October informing members of available pamphlets and books and of classes scheduled on "Parent-Child Relationships."

Summary

By the completion of the preparatory phase of problem solving the group will have moved from an awareness of the problem through two phases and a series of steps culminating in the selection of a course of action. If all of the procedures and process-es have been adequately performed by the problem-solving group, then it will have not only made a wise selection, but it will have done so in a manner that has ensured a high level of cohesion and commit-ment. Furthermore, the members of the group are quite likely to support and, if appropriate, to contri-bute time, talent, energy, and effort to the next phase of the problem-solving process. The last major phase of integrated problem solving will consist of imple-menting the selected course of action and evaluating the process or the outcome.

6 The Implementation and Evaluation Phase: Act and Review

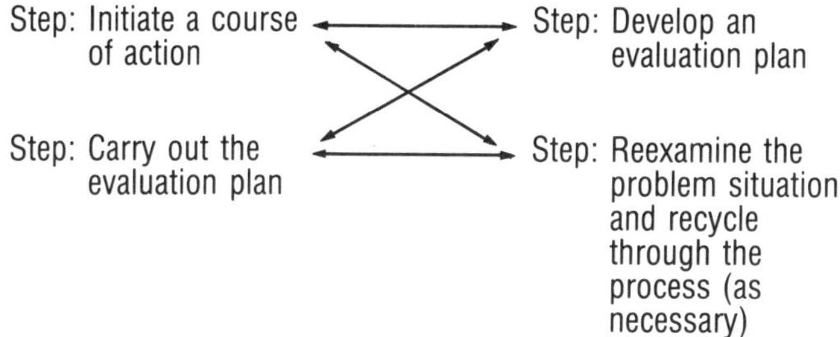

Introduction

There are four component procedures to the implementation and evaluation phase: developing an evaluation plan, initiating a course of action, carrying out the evaluation plan, and reexamining the situation in order to determine whether or not to go through the process again. The sequence of these component procedures is quite variable because of the variability of the types of evaluation that can be utilized. Different types of evaluation and different combinations of types of evaluation create a number of different procedural options for the problem-solving group. Thus, rather than following the format of the last two chapters, this chapter will first consider implementation in general, then present an overview of evaluation, and finally describe the six basic patterns in the implementation and evaluation phase.

Perspective implementation

The implementation aspect of integrated problem solving involves carrying out the action plan developed in the preparatory phase. The implementation procedures include preparing the congregation for change, initiating a course of action, altering the intervention as necessary, and completing the intervention.

Preparing the congregation for change

The typical congregation has a set or "frozen" way of behaving in terms of any given area in which a crisis, problem, or need occurs. The action to be taken in response to the need for change will require some alteration in the "frozen" behavior of the congregation. Thus, some aspects of the ongoing life of the congregation must be figuratively "unfrozen" in order to enable the change to occur. The procedure of unfreezing requires that the appropriate people in the congregation be informed about the nature of the problem, the steps that have been taken, and the nature of the future actions that will occur. In some instances announcements in the church bulletin, newsletters, and in various meetings are helpful. For some major changes, a congregational meeting may be in order. In some cases a training effort is required. The purpose of this procedure is to prepare the congregation for change. In effect, the unfreezing process helps to create a readiness for a "positive disintegration" of certain congregational programs and activities so that new programs and activities can be set in place as a response to the challenge of change.

Initiate a course of action

Once the congregation has been unfrozen and is ready for change, the actual change-oriented action can begin. As noted in Chapter 2, the action may be structural, technological, or behavioral in quality. The schedule may call for an all-out, full-speed-ahead-type effort or the schedule may be slower and more deliberate. Action may be directed toward dealing with a congregation-wide problem, such as a serious financial problem. On the other hand, the action may be directed toward a given system within the congregation, e.g., the choir, the Sunday school, or the confirmation class. Sometimes the change-oriented action involves smaller segments of the congregation such as a single family, a couple, or an individual. Three keys to success in implementing the action plan are as follows:

1. Provide adequate resources for the people responsible for carrying out the action plan:
   - Finances
   - Time
   - Talent

- Space
- People
- Materials
- Training

2. Monitor progress in carrying out the plan.
3. Follow the plan unless there is clear evidence that the plan should be altered.

Alter the intervention as necessary

Sometimes as the change-oriented action is monitored, it becomes evident that the original action plan should be altered. In such a case the problem-solving group should reconsider the plan and revise it in light of the feedback received during the monitoring efforts. Having revised the plan, the implementation (action) efforts can then proceed according to the new revised action plan. This revising of the action plan and the subsequent implementation should be repeated until a plan and a subsequent course of action results in an adequate resolution of the problem situation.

A perspective on evaluation

In many instances, after identifying a problem and hastily considering a few alternative courses of action, the problem-solving group will quickly move to the implementation phase of problem solving. In most congregations, problem-solving and decision-making groups either omit evaluation or perform a quick evaluation. Since they move so rapidly into the implementation phase, they at first appear to be very efficient. In reality, however, a problem-solving group that has not carried out the proper foundational work and has not adequately built in an evaluation component is apt to be inefficient and ineffective in the long run. It is apt to decide to take the wrong course of action, or else its lack of adequate preparation causes many problems in the implementation phase such as resentment, bitterness, conflicts, sabotage, and the like. Moreover, unless the problem-solving group builds in a good evaluation component, it cannot know how effective or efficient its efforts have been. Furthermore, without a good evaluation a problem-solving group cannot adequately examine its own efforts and make the necessary corrections to improve the way it functions in the future.

One of the major strengths of integrated problem solving is that while it may initially appear to be an involved, cumbersome process, in reality it saves time and effort in the long run. The inclusion of an evaluation component to the problem-solving process adds additional steps. It is tempting to either omit or short-cut evaluation. In light of the above line of thought, however, a well-thought-out and well-implemented evaluation effort improves the overall results.

Evaluation is the least understood and most neglected aspect of the problem-solving process. Sometimes evaluation is omitted. More typically, the committee or other type of working group quickly and haphazardly "eyeballs" evaluation at the end of the intervention. Two of the many good reasons for including systematic evaluation in the problem-solving process are: (1) it enables the group to know how well it has carried out its mission, and (2) it can provide helpful information to enable the group to improve the way it functions. In this light it is important to distinguish between two types of evaluation: *outcome evaluation* and *process evaluation*. Outcome evaluation assesses the extent to which the goals of the group are met, i.e., how the intervention "turned out." Process evaluation, on the other hand, assesses how well the problem-solving group functions as a group and/or how well the intermediate steps in the total process contributed to the final outcome.

The evaluational aspect of problem solving may be conceived of in terms of three major steps. First, an evaluation plan is developed. Next, the evaluation plan is carried out by evaluating (1) the outcome results of the implementation (action phase) and (2) how well the problem-solving group functioned in accomplishing the various aspects of the action phase. Last, the group reexamines the problem situation in order to determine whether the problem has been adequately solved or whether further action is required.

Developing an evaluation plan

The essence of this step is that the problem-solving group develop an evaluation plan to assess some or all of the following: the effectiveness of each action step in implementing the plan, the degree to which the desired outcomes were achieved, and/or the overall quality of the interactions within the problem-solving group. The basic procedures in this step are as follows:

1. Determine whether to carry out an outcome evaluation, process evaluation, or both types

of evaluation. The evaluation plan may be developed either in conjunction with the overall plan or it may be developed after the overall plan has been developed but before the plan is completely implemented.

2. Create a time line for carrying out the evaluation plan.
3. Determine the evaluation responsibilities of each group member.

Although it is beyond the scope of this book to describe the details of this step, the interested reader may refer to Morris and Shashkin (*Organization Behavior in Action*) or any other basic evaluation text for the specifics of the procedures in this step. As is the case throughout integrated problem solving, it is important in this step to carry out the procedures by involving all group members, sharing the concerns of group members, resolving differences among group members, and developing both consensus and commitment to the evaluation effort. Although this step is often omitted from the problem-solving process, evaluation is critical, for without it the problem-solving group cannot know how well it has accomplished its task. Moreover, without evaluation the group cannot systematically alter how it functions in order to improve its future problem-solving efforts.

Carrying out the evaluation plan

In this step the evaluation plan is implemented. Each step of the overall action plan and/or the degree to which the goals were met may be evaluated. The problem-solving group may choose to evaluate its own processes by assessing the participation patterns of each group member, evaluating the degree of openness and support between and among group members, and/or evaluating what the group has learned about the process of integrated problem solving.

Reexamining the problem situation and recycling through the process as necessary

To the extent that the problem-solving effort has been successful, the problem will have been eliminated. Typically, however, the successful problem-solving effort has reduced the frequency, severity, or duration of the problem. Problems, crises, and needs are rarely eliminated completely. By reexamining the problem, the group can determine whether further action is warranted. If no further action is needed, then the problem-solving group will either disband or move on to deal with another situation. If, on the other hand, the problem has not been adequately resolved, then the group should recycle through the total problem-solving process.

The implementation and evaluation phase: six patterns

As noted at the beginning of this chapter, integrated problem solving is a linear or straight-line method in the readiness and preparatory phases, but the sequence of steps is quite variable in the implementation and evaluation phase. Figure 6-1 illustrates each of six possible alternative patterns for the implementation and evaluation phase. Patterns A, B, and C each call for developing an evaluation plan before initiating action. To be sure, if there is no critical need to bring about change quickly, it is preferable to develop the evaluation plan before initiating the action. Patterns A, B, and C may be a luxury that some congregational problem-solving groups may not be able to choose. Pattern A depicts the most thorough approach, for it includes both process evaluation and outcome evaluation as well as preinterventional evaluation planning. Two related sequences involving preinterventional planning are represented by Pattern B (which employs only outcome evaluation) and Pattern C (which employs only process evaluation).

If the problem-solving group cannot take time to develop a preinterventional evaluation plan, the evaluation plan can be developed simultaneously with the initiation of the action. Pattern D illustrates a simultaneous initiation of action and evaluation planning effort that includes both outcome and process evaluation. Pattern E also illustrates parallel initiation of action and evaluation planning, followed by outcome evaluation. Finally, in Pattern F there is parallel initiation of action and evaluation planning followed by process evaluation. The use of only process evaluation is not recommended under normal problem-solving circumstances because it does not allow the group to determine how well it has accomplished its goals.

Regardless of the sequence of activities carried out by the problem-solving group, the implementation and evaluation phase ends when a reexamination of the problem situation reveals that goals have been met and the problem has either been eliminated or adequately reduced.

Figure 6-1
Six Evaluation Patterns

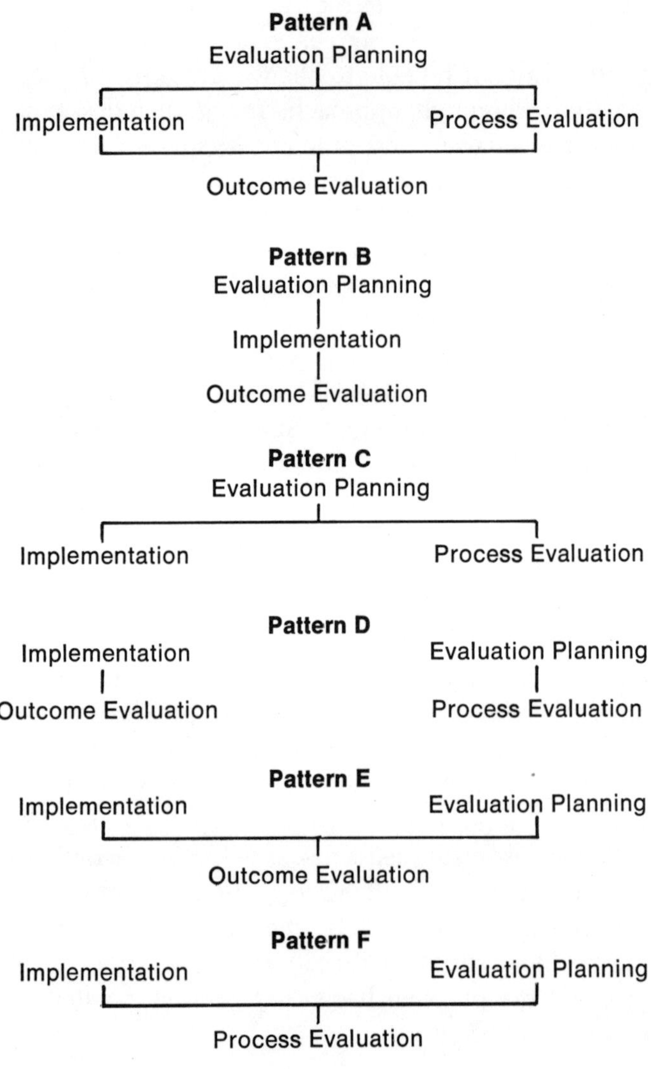

Summary

With the completion of the implementation and evaluation phase, the process of integrated problem solving is complete. This method integrates the best elements of scientific problem solving with compatible problem solving elements that are spiritual in quality. As noted throughout the description of this method, the process consists of three major phases, each of which is implemented through a series of steps with related procedures and processes. In its pure form integrated problem solving looks long and complex. In fact, however, by building in the critical readiness and preparatory activities, it has the potential for being more efficient and effective than other methods employed by congregational working groups. In some instances, it may be appropriate for the congregational working group to employ all aspects of this method for the problem-solving aspects of its work. In other cases it would probably be more appropriate for the congregational working group to incorporate selected aspects of this method into the method currently being employed. Only a rare situation will not benefit by applying some aspect of integrated problem solving.

Part 3: Variations

This final section will consider some of the many variations in regard to how working groups within a congregation respond to the challenge of change. Given the wide range of circumstances, personalities, and styles involved in the functioning of these groups, it naturally follows there should be a great deal of variability in how these groups function.

The variations are both qualitative and quantitative. Working groups within church congregations vary along many dimensions such as leadership, goals, communication, cohesion, task-orientedness, and formality of style. These groups also vary in terms of the types of balance they develop in such areas as spiritual versus secular emphases, change versus stability, and the roles and functions of clergy and laity.

The phenomenon of change is both real and critical for the Christian church as a societal institution and for vitality in the ongoing life of the local congregation. In this light, the purpose of this final portion of the book is to place the phenomenon of change, the local congregation, problem solving, and the mission of the local congregation into better perspective. The intent of the local congregation is to demonstrate its love of God and humankind in its own unique way. Given the challenge of change, the local congregation is indeed blessed with a unique opportunity to express its identity and commitment in the form of service.

Faith and good works, love and service, identity and commitment, response and action—these components coupled with a functional set of ministries, activities, and programs can enable a congregation to serve God and humankind in a world that is in desperate need of the redeeming message the Christian church offers.

7 Variations in the Method

The theme of this book has been that the church as a societal institution and the local congregation are standing at a crossroads and that they both must make a set of critical decisions and embark upon a course of action in response to the challenge of change. Part 1 presented a perspective on the nature of change and also highlighted the nature of the challenge of change. Part 2 described integrated problem solving as a possible technique for helping the local congregation respond to change.

Such techniques are often proposed as if they were formulas or recipes. The steps in the process and the procedures are "carved in stone," with the expectation the method will be used according to the exact formula or recipe prescribed. In one sense this is true in the case of integrated problem solving. One way of using this method follows the strict series of phases, steps, procedures, and processes summarized in Part 2. More probably, however, a problem-solving group that is aware of this method will adapt it to fit its own character and unique situation. Human beings, especially when functioning within the context of groups and group dynamics, tend to alter or modify the neat and tidy prescriptions offered by others. In this light, the following points appear noteworthy:

1. Integrated problem solving as described in Part 2 has been presented as an "ideal" type of intervention.
2. Some congregational working groups may elect to employ this method in its pure form.
3. Other congregational working groups will undoubtedly modify or mold this basic method to conform with the ongoing style of that group.
4. Some congregational working groups may determine that this method is inappropriate for their use.

This chapter will consider some basic dimensions of the problem-solving process, pointing out the many variations in how congregational working groups may function as they respond to change. These variations do not represent a repudiation of integrated problem solving. Rather, the variations are presented as valid options that can be linked with aspects of integrated problem solving. Although there are many variations in the basic steps used in problem solving, most approaches follow a basic pattern:

1. Become aware of a problem.
2. Define the nature of the problem.
3. Consider alternative courses of action.

4. Select a course of action.
5. Carry out the intervention.
6. Evaluate the process or the outcome.
7. Recycle as necessary.

Variations in the goals dimension

Aside from the huge variety of specific goals, problem-solving groups vary in terms of the types of goals they espouse. Groups with remedial goals seek to solve problems that already exist. Groups with preventive goals attempt to avoid problems. Groups with enrichment goals do not deal with problems at all. Rather, they try to build on the positive aspects of congregational life. Viewing goals somewhat differently, congregational working groups may seek long-term or short-term goals. The unique goals of each problem-solving group will, in effect, determine the general direction in which that group will go. The other dimensions of problem solving, however, will determine the means by which the group achieves its goals.

The style dimension

The two lists below delineate the contrasting styles that can characterize a congregational working group engaged in problem solving.

Systematic	Unsystematic
Conflicting	Harmonious
Cooperative	Competitive
Open	Closed
Cohesive	Fragmented
Leader-centered	Group-centered

Friendly	Unfriendly
Serious	Casual
Open communication	Restricted communication
High performance standards	Low performance standards
Formal	Informal

The leadership dimension

Without a doubt, the single most important factor that influences how a congregational working group will function is the nature of its leadership. The formal and informal leaders in effect set the initial style and greatly influence the content and the process aspects of the group. The behaviors of group members are largely a response to the behaviors of the group leader(s). Figure 7-1 depicts the triangle of leadership in terms of three basic leadership components.

The *directive type* of leader is one who attempts to control the other members of group toward group interactions and outcomes deemed desirable by the leader. On the other hand, the *collaborative type* of leader becomes a co-worker with the other group members, jointly determining the nature of group interactions and group outcomes or goals with them. The *facilitative type* of leader functions as enabler, i.e., one who helps the group develop its own group interactions and determine its own goals.

A group leader who employs one leadership approach may be either a pure collaborator (1), a pure director (2) or a pure enabler (3). Some leaders (eclectic leaders) employ equal combinations of two approaches (4, 5, and 6). A type of

Figure 7-1
The Triangle of Leadership Approaches

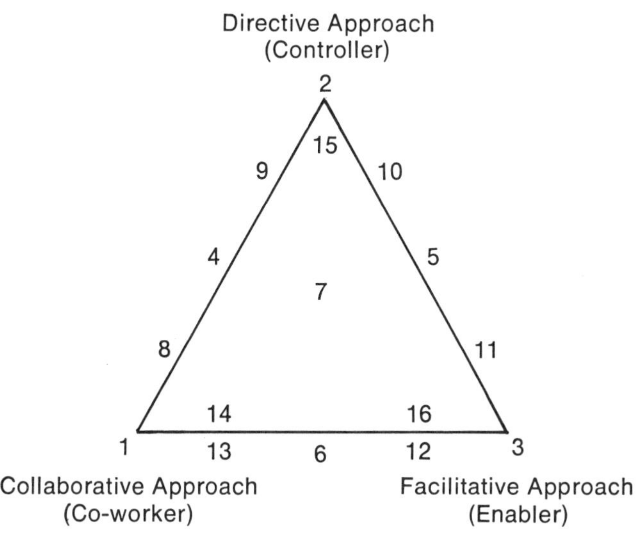

group leader who employs approximately equal amounts of collaborative, directive, and facilitative approaches is represented by position 7 on the triangle of leadership. Numbers 8, 9, 10, 11, 12, and 13 represent eclectic leadership approaches that employ unequal amounts of two different leadership approaches. Numbers 15, 16, and 17 in the leadership triangle represent different amounts of the three leadership approaches.

Each leadership approach envisions that the group members will react in a complementary manner to the approach of the leaders. For example, to the extent that a group leader is directive (controlling), it is helpful if group members comply with the expectations of the leader. To the extent that the leader is collaborative, it is helpful if the other group members are willing to work with the leader in a cooperative or coactive manner. To the extent that the leader uses a facilitative approach, it is helpful if the other group members respond by taking the initiative in developing their own group goals and the actions or means to achieve those goals. If the approach of the group leader and the response of the group members "fit" well, then the problem-solving group is apt to function well. When the approach of the leader and response of the group members does not "fit" well, i.e., are not complementary, then the group is not apt to be either effective or efficient in its operation.

The role dimension

In order for a problem-solving group to function well, its members must adequately perform two sets of role behaviors: group-task roles and group-building (maintenance) roles. Again, groups vary greatly in the ways they carry out these roles.

1. **Group-task roles.** These are the roles required for selecting and carrying out a group task.
   - *Initiating activity:* proposing solutions; suggesting new ideas, new definitions of the problem, new attacks on the problem, or new organization of material.
   - *Seeking information:* questioning, seeking clarification, or making suggestions; requesting additional information or facts.

- *Seeking opinion:* looking for an expression of feeling about something from the members; seeking clarification of values, suggestions, or ideas.
- *Giving information:* offering facts or generalizations; relating one's own experience to the group to illustrate a point.
- *Giving opinion:* stating an opinion or belief concerning a suggestion or one of several suggestions, particularly concerning its value rather than its factual basis.
- *Elaborating:* clarifying, giving examples, or developing meanings; trying to envision how a proposal might work out if adopted.
- *Coordinating:* showing relationships among various ideas or suggestions; trying to pull ideas and suggestions together; trying to draw together activities of various subgroups or members.
- *Summarizing:* pulling together related ideas or suggestions; restating suggestions after the group has discussed them.
- *Testing feasibility:* making applications of suggestions to real situations; examining practicality and workability of ideas; pre-evaluating decisions.

2. **Group-building (maintenance) roles.** These are the social-emotional functions required for strengthening and maintaining group life and activities.

- *Encouraging:* being friendly, warm, responsive to others; praising others and their ideas; agreeing with and accepting contributions of others.
- *Gate keeping:* trying to make it possible for

another member to make a contribution to the group.

- *Standard setting:* expressing standards for group to use in choosing its content or procedures or in evaluating its decisions; reminding group to avoid decisions that conflict with group standards.
- *Following:* going along with decisions of the group; somewhat passively accepting ideas of others.
- *Expressing group feeling:* summarizing what group feeling is sensed to be; describing reactions of the group to ideas or solutions.

3. **Both group-task and group-building roles.** These are roles that may fulfill both task and social-emotional functions.
   - *Evaluating:* submitting group decisions or accomplishments to comparison with group standards; measuring accomplishments against goals.
   - *Diagnosing:* determining sources of difficulties, appropriate steps to take next, or the main blocks to progress.
   - *Testing for consensus:* tentatively asking for group opinions in order to find out if the group is nearing consensus on a decision; sending up trial balloons to test group opinions.
   - *Mediating:* harmonizing; conciliatory differences in points of view; making compromise solutions.

4. **Some types of nonfunctional behavior.** The following behaviors can be interpreted differently by different members of the group. What may appear, for example, to one member as "blocking" may seem to another a needed effort toward "testing feasibility."

- *Being aggressive:* working for status by criticizing or blaming others, showing hostility against the group or some individual, deflating the ego or status of others. (Examples: gossip, ridicule, sarcasm, bullying, physical aggression, etc., by either students or teacher.)
- *Blocking:* interfering with the progress of the group by going off on a tangent; citing personal experiences unrelated to the problem; arguing too much on a point; rejecting ideas without consideration.
- *Competing:* vying with others to produce the best idea, to talk the most, to play the most roles, or to gain favor with the leader.
- *Seeking sympathy:* trying to induce other group members to be sympathetic to one's problems or misfortunes; deploring one's own situation or disparaging one's own ideas to gain support.
- *Seeking recognition:* attempting to call attention to oneself by loud or excessive talking, extreme ideas, or unusual behavior.
- *Withdrawing:* acting indifferently or passively; resorting to excessive formality; doodling; whispering to others; wandering from the subject.

The tactical dimension

The tactical dimension refers to nature of the phases, steps, or stages in the problem-solving process. There are both quantitative and qualitative aspects to this dimension. For example, in the most simple tactic, a problem is sensed, the leader decides on a course of action, the action is announced to the group, and the group willingly complies by getting down to the work of implementing the decision made by a leader. Most problem-solving methods are somewhat longer and more complex than this example. Integrated problem solving is rather long and complex in terms of the many phases and steps in the tactical dimension. Any problem-solving method can become very long and complex in terms of the tactical dimension if, for example, the group becomes involved in internal conflicts, misinterpretations of communication, sabotage, and/or hurt feelings.

The procedural dimension

The procedural dimension of problem solving refers to the specific procedures or techniques utilized by the leader(s) and other group members. The procedures listed below are categorized in terms of their relationship to the leadership triangle.

1. Procedures (techniques) related to the directive (controlling) approach:

Commanding	Demanding
Urging	Exhorting
Warning	Telling
Teaching	Ordering
Convincing	Training
Advising	Directing
Coercing	Suggesting
Offering options	Selling
Prompting	Opposing
Approving	Warning
Confronting	Interrupting
Redirecting	Disagreeing
Agreeing	Blocking

2. Procedures (techniques) related to the collaborative (co-worker) approach:

Joint goal setting — Joint data analysis
Joint planning — Perception checking
Joint scheduling — Sentiment testing
Brainstorming — Negotiating
Joint needs analysis (assessment) — Joint problem solving
Joint evaluation

3. Procedures (techniques) related to the facilitative (enabling) approach:

   A. Strengthening procedures

Providing resources — Illustration
Summarizing — Interpretation
Questioning (probe) — Reflection
Relaxation techniques — Paradoxical intention
Clarifying — Prayer

   B. Supporting procedures

Acceptance — Bolstering
Encouragement — Inspiring
Understanding — Caring
Prayer — Touching
Reassurance — Listening
Approval — Biblical therapy
Nurturing

Summary

Working groups typically do not use any problem-solving method in its pure form. Rather, they adapt one or more methods to suit their own unique needs and circumstances. This chapter has presented six basic dimensions of the problem-solving process and has summarized some of the many variations in the basic pattern that most problem-solving groups employ. The variations described in this chapter constitute some of the many options available to the congregation as it deals with problem-solving aspects of its work. These variations make problem solving a rich and useful technology.

8 Developing a Proper Balance

Introduction

There are both qualitative and quantitative aspects to the problem-solving process. Thus far the thrust of this book has been directed toward describing the qualitative aspects of problem solving. This chapter will extend the discussion of variations in the problem-solving process but will emphasize the quantitative aspects of those differences. The basic intent here is to discuss patterns of problem-solving components in terms of how much of each component is necessary to provide an appropriate balance for any given problem-solving group.

Spiritual-secular balance

As working groups within local congregations function within the problem-solving aspects of their work, they vary greatly in respect to their relative emphasis on spiritual and secular matters. These groups are neither totally spiritual nor totally secular; rather, by their very nature, working groups within the congregation are simultaneously spiritual and secular, i.e., spiritual-secular. Working groups vary qualitatively and quantitatively in their spiritual-secular balance. While there are many aspects of the qualitative and quantitative spiritual-secular balance, this discussion can consider only a few of them. The spiritual quality of each working group is derived in part from the basic theological stance of the congregation in general, in part from the style of the working group, and in part from the theological (spiritual) orientation of each member of the group. From a quantitative standpoint, congregational working groups vary in terms of their relative focus or emphasis on spiritual and secular matters.

If a problem-solving group utilizes a primarily secular balance, it will tend to view its task in terms of employing secular technologies to solve church problems. From a group dynamics vantage point, it will function in a manner similar to a working group in any secular organization such as a business, an industry, or a civic organization. The local church is seen as merely another organization in which secular technologies such as those listed below may be harnessed to bring about organizational change:

1. Computerization of records.
2. Utilization of advanced budgeting or accounting methods.
3. Application of modern management approaches.
4. Employment of secularly-oriented advertisement or public relations approaches.

5. Utilization of time management techniques for optimizing the productivity of staff members.
6. Employment of sophisticated performance appraisal methods for evaluating the work of staff members.

On the other hand, a focus that is more secular than spiritual typically acknowledges the spiritual aspect, but only in a minimal way. Often this style involves beginning a meeting with a prayer, Bible reading, or brief devotional activity. These activities, however, tend to be ceremonial in quality. For example, a stewardship committee operating in this manner might begin with a brief devotional ceremony and then quickly get down to the "important business of fund raising."

In a balanced focus, the working group will use an approximately equal emphasis on spiritual and secular matters. For example, a committee of Sunday school teachers selecting new curriculum materials through a balanced approach would not only evaluate those materials in terms of their educational or classroom merit but would also evaluate in some depth the extent to which the materials conform to that group's position on spiritual issues.

If a congregational working group utilizes a balance that is more spiritual than secular, it will have a proportionally higher emphasis on the spiritual aspects of its work. An illustration of this stance would be a building committee that in planning the design for a new church sanctuary emphasizes the spiritual and/or liturgical aspects of how the new sanctuary should function. This group would deal in depth with the nature and dynamics of congregational worship rather than with the architectural aspects of sanctuary design. Also, a primarily spiritual emphasis will view its tasks as essentially spiritual. A young couples support group utilizing this type of balance would probably emphasize Bible study and prayer and deemphasize social activities and psychologically oriented topics for discussion. While it is true that various types of congregational working groups might naturally tend to lean to one type of spiritual-secular balance, it is equally true that any congregational working group could appropriately utilize any type of balance along the spiritual-secular continuum.

Within the spiritual domain there is another matter of balance that deals not with the relative amounts of spiritual and secular emphasis but rather with the types and amounts of spiritually based activities any given work group utilizes. A congregational working group has a potentially wide range of spiritual activities that it might employ:

1. Bible reading
2. Reading various types of religious materials
3. Bible study
4. Devotional studies
5. Testimonials
6. Religious music
7. Spiritually-oriented audiovisual aids
8. Object lessons

Given the large number of different types of spiritual activities that any given congregational working group might employ and the differing relative emphases that might be placed on each of the many possible combinations of these activities, there is an incredible spiritual richness that a group might either draw upon and utilize or else reject as not appropriate for its use. The matter of spiritual-secular balance is further complicated by how the group decides to use the spiritual and secular components available for its use. Spiritual components, for example, can be used for a variety of purposes:

1. To comfort and support group members.
2. To guide the decision making and action of the group.
3. To help prepare the group to carry on its work.
4. To open the group to the work of the Holy Spirit.
5. To instruct, enlighten, or inform group members.
6. To provide an adequate perspective for the work of the group.
7. To build group cohesion.
8. To strengthen the resolve of the group when it meets obstacles in its work.

Last, each problem-solving meeting has three distinct stages: an opening phase, a working phase, and a closing phase. Given these three phases in each meeting of the problem-solving group and given the many specific spiritual and secular components, there is a great deal of variability in the place in each meeting in which each spiritual and each secular component is utilized by the problem-solving group.

The balance between the roles of clergy and laity

In the long history of the Christian church there has been a traditionally strong dichotomy between the roles of the clergy *(kleros)* and the lay people *(laos)*. The traditional distinction between the roles of these two groups are contrasted below:

Clergy	**Laity**
Leaders	Followers
Helpers	Helpees
Producers	Consumers
Performers	Spectators

In this traditional view the word *minister* (derived from the Latin word *ministerium*) is closely related to the Greek word *diakonia,* and the root meaning of both of these words is "to serve." Based on the traditional concept of *ekklesia,* the "called out," this traditional view delineates the clergy as the "called" ones —those called to serve. The clergy are called to serve the people. They are viewed as shepherds; the congregation is the flock. Based on the example of Christ and his disciples, the Christian church has traditionally relied upon the clergy to perform the key roles as the active agents in the life of the congregation. This view envisions congregational members as the rather passive "flock." A work analysis of all of the tasks that must be performed in the ongoing life of the congregation, however, reveals that it is not realistic or feasible to expect any one or two people to carry out all of those congregational functions.

An alternative to the traditional balance between the roles of the clergy and the laity is emerging. This emerging view flows in part from the image and pattern of the New Testament church and stems from the basic conception of the congregation as a priesthood of all believers. In this emerging view, each Christian has the potential for engaging in six different types of ministries:

1. The ministry of proclamation (preaching)
2. The ministry of teaching
3. The ministry of worship
4. The ministry of fellowship
5. The ministry of service
6. The ministry of witness

This concept of each congregational member engaging in a series of ministries does not negate the role of the clergy. Rather, it delineates a more strategic role for clergy. Clergy *lead* and *feed* the congregation through such roles as preaching, leading worship services, administering the sacraments, and officiating at weddings and funerals. Most of the other roles and functions of the church are totally or primarily the responsibility of the laity. In this view the "called out" *(ekklesia)* consist of both clergy and laity. All Christians are called to serve as ministers.

One important aspect of the challenge of change is the need for the local congregation to reexamine the qualitative and quantitative balance in the roles of clergy and laity. Given the many unique types of missions and circumstances among Christian congregations, there are many different appropriate types of balance in how the congregations pattern their ministries.

The balance between ministries and programs

In order to achieve its mission the typical congregation employs both ministries and programs. As noted above, a ministry may be conceived of as some type of unique *response* to a *call* (from God). Often the concept of ministry is linked with stewardship, i.e., the Christian's use of talents and resources that have been given by God. The emphasis here is contributing one's unique talents and resources to the work of the congregation. A program, on the other hand, is typically conceived of as a technological approach for accomplishing the mission of a congregation. Some typical types of congregational programs include evangelism programs, stewardship programs, and membership programs. Typically the church leadership senses a problem and thereafter develops a program, i.e., a technologically based effort to alleviate that problem.

Change efforts that primarily employ either ministries or programs often fall short of the mark. Many congregations, for example, are overprogrammed and use too small a participatory base from their membership. A small number of members attempt to "carry the load" of implementing the programs of the congregation. This small group of members become overworked, overburdened, and overstressed. In time, the results of these efforts are very predictable. The small group of dependable, hard-working members get burned out. They then feel a mixture of guilt, resentment, and alienation, and in the long run the programs falter and fail.

At first glance, an extreme reliance on the stewardship-ministry approach seems like an appealing alternative to the overreliance on congregational programming. A major shortcoming, however, in an extreme stewardship-ministerial effort to deal with change, is that without programs it is very difficult to coordinate the many unique and idiosyncratic efforts of individual member's ministries. A type of balance advocated implicitly throughout this book has been as follows: *Stewardship,* planned and developed by a systematic *problem-solving* effort, can result in a coordinated set of individual clergy and lay *ministries* and congregational *programs.*

The balance between formality and informality

One of the more pervasive trends in our society is a marked change from what sociologists term a *Gemeinschaft* type of society to a *Gesellschaft* type of society. The main features of these two types of societies in terms of the basic qualities of human interaction are summarized below.

GEMEINSCHAFT SOCIETY (Traditionalism)	GESELLSCHAFT SOCIETY (Modernism)
Informal	Formal
Long-term relationships	Short-term relationships
Interpersonal involvement	Interpersonal alienation
Intensive interactions	Casual interactions

Like other societal organizations, congregations have mirrored the above patterns of change in how their members relate to one another. In large and small congregations alike there has been a marked tendency to develop structural and human interaction patterns increasingly characterized by such terms as bureaucratized, specialized, formalized, segmentalized, etc. The term *modernization* has been increasingly used to denote this total pattern of structuring an organization and to denote the emerging pattern of formal, cordial-but-distant interpersonal relationships among congregational members. The evidence is quite clear: much of the progress of humankind in the past can be traced directly to the increase in task efficiency and task effectiveness of "modernized" organizations. But the evidence is also clear that the recent accelerated rate of change has in large part negated the ability of modernized bureaucracies to deal with change. The local congregation is one example of a bureaucratic type of organization that is plagued by many problems stemming from the forces of change.

It would appear foolhardy to reject all aspects of modernity and its characteristic formal structures of bureaucratic organization. Yet it is clear that in many congregations some types of changes in structure and in the patterns of human interaction seem to be warranted. Some congregations are developing small, informal subgroupings of their members within which people can establish relationships that approximate those of *Gemeinschaft* societies.

Summary

This chapter has highlighted a few of the many types of balance that must be developed within the ongoing life of a congregation. Obviously, there is no single formula for developing an appropriate set of balances for all congregations. Conditions and circumstances vary. There are wide variations in needs, preferences, capacities, and styles. It may be the case that some congregations create a set of appropriate balances without any type of systematic effort. More probably, however, an absence of systematic effort will result in a set of imbalances. Systematic problem solving can be the pivotal activity in developing an appropriate set of qualitative and quantitative balances that will enable the congregation to fulfill its mission.

Some final thoughts

It is one thing to *believe* that we are God's people, but it is difficult to *be* his people.

It is often our intention to *seek* the kingdom of God, but we often *restrict* the work of the Holy Spirit.

It is often noted that we should *bear fruit*, but it requires diligence and effort to be a *bearer of fruit*.

It is easy to say that we should be a *light* to the world, but it is hard to *shine*.

It is common to think that God's people are the *salt* of the earth, but it is difficult to *flavor* the lives of other people.

It has been said that we should be *yeast*, but we often miss opportunities to *leaven* and *enrich* the lives of those around us.

It is easy to be *familiar with* the promises in the Word, but it is difficult to *stand on* those promises.

And who is my neighbor?

Bibliography

Abdon, Donald. *Training and Equipping the Saints.* Indianapolis, Indiana: Parish Leadership Seminars, 1977.

Accola, Louis. "Types of Goals for Working Groups in the Congregation." Unpublished handout for leadership workshop held in Champaign, Illinois, 1980.

Fisher, Wallace E. *A New Climate for Leadership.* Nashville: Parthenon, 1976. Out of print.

Haas, Eugene, and Drabeck, Thomas E. *Complex Organizations.* New York: Macmillan, 1973.

Lippitt, Gordon and Schmidt, Warren. "Crises in Developing Organizations." *Harvard Business Review,* November-December, 1967.

Minear, Paul S. *Images of the Church in the New Testament.* Philadelphia: Westminster, 1970.

Morris, William C., and Shashkin, Marshal. *Organization Behavior in Action: Skill Building Experiences.* New York: West Publishing Co., 1976.

Snyder, Howard A. *Community of the King.* Downers Grove, Illinois: InterVarsity Press, 1977.

Tannenbaum, R., and Schmidt, W. "How to Choose a Leadership Pattern." *Harvard Business Review,* May-June, 1973.